Kitten
Care and Training

An Owner's Guide To

A HAPPY HEALTHY PET

Howell Book House

Howell Book House
A Simon & Schuster Macmillan Company
1633 Broadway
New York, NY 10019

MACMILLAN is a registered trademark of Macmillan, Inc.

Library of Congress Cataloging-in-Publication data
Shojai, Amy, 1956–
Kitten care and training : an owner's guide to a happy healthy pet/by Amy Shojai.
p. cm.
Includes bibliographical references.
ISBN 0-87605-392-4
1. Kittens. 2. Cats. I. Title.
SF447.S48   1996
636.8'07—dc20   95-49504
                    CIP

ISBN 0-87605-392-4

Manufactured in the United States of America

Series Director: Dominique De Vito
Series Assistant Director: Ariel Cannon
Book Design: Michele Laseau
Cover Design: Iris Jeromnimon
Cover Photo by Cheryl Primeau; kitten by Pets by Paulette
Paulette Braun/Pets by Paulette: 4, 15, 75, 93, 146
Joan Balzarini: 17, 21, 27, 49, 77, 78, 80, 82, 113, 125, 127
Mary Bloom: 41
Cheryl Primeau: 5, 29, 35, 38–39, 61, 62, 76, 103, 104, 115, 130, 139, 142
Susan Rezy: 42, 43, 53, 58, 118, 121
Judith Strom: 64, 108, 110, 141
Jean Wentworth: 2–3, 6, 7, 9, 11, 18, 23, 26, 32, 34, 36, 40, 45, 46, 54, 65, 66, 68, 70, 91,
100–101, 102, 105, 106, 111, 128, 135, 136, 137, 140, 144
Production Team: Trudy Brown, Jama Carter, Kathleen Caulfield, Trudy Coler,
   Amy De Angelis, Pete Fornatale, Matt Hannafin, Kathy Iwasaki, Vic Peterson,
   Terri Sheehan, Marvin Van Tiem, and Kathleen Varanese

ISBN 978-1-68442-231-9 (pbk.)

Contents

part one

Welcome
to the
World
of Your
Kitten

chapter 1

The
Kitten's
Ancestry

Congratulations on the new arrival! Nothing prompts bigger smiles or greater delight than welcoming a fuzzy new baby into the family. Your kitten's batting paws, playful pounces, and insistent mews are not only endearing; they also reflect an aristocratic heritage. Cats purred their way into human hearts many thousands of years ago, and they have been enriching our lives ever since.

In the Beginning

Cats got their start long before humans were on the scene. *Miacids*, the earliest forebear of modern cats, evolved during the

5

mid-Paleocene epoch about 61 million years ago. The earliest Miacids were small but ferocious carnivores that lived in forests and probably looked something like today's shrews. Experts believe they were equally at home on the ground or climbing trees, and they probably had retractable claws, like modern kitties.

A variety of catlike creatures sprang from the pint-size Miacids and flourished across most of the world. Miacids became the founding father for all modern carnivores, including the bear (*Ursidae*), weasel and badger (*Mustelidae*), hyena (*Hyaenidae*), civet, genet and mongoose (*Viverridae*), raccoon (*Procyonidae*), dog, fox and wolf (*Canidae*) and, of course, the entire cat family (*Felidae*).

The Felidae family tree is approximately three million years old.

But cats didn't start looking much like cats until about 12 million years ago when creatures resembling today's felines first prowled and growled across the world. Nine million years later, the *Felidae* family tree branched into the major cat types we currently recognize, and all modern-day cats, both big and small, evolved from these first felines.

Panthera are the big roaring cats: the lions, tigers, leopards and jaguars. Two big cats are so unique they have their own genus: *Acinonyx* for the cheetah and *Neofelis* for the clouded leopard. *Felis* embraces more than twenty-eight kinds of small cats, including cougars, bobcats, twenty-three subspecies of wildcats, and domestic cats like your kitten.

Cat Meets Human

Cats of all sizes were already on the scene when humans first appeared. In the beginning, people probably competed with cats for food, and no doubt they sometimes even stalked each other. Early man envied the feline's success, and he celebrated her hunting prowess in prehistoric cave drawings of lions. Cat amulets indicate that feline cults glorified the cat in Egypt as early as the 6th Dynasty.

Exactly when cats stepped over the threshold and became domesticated is still open to debate. Some experts believe domestication may have begun as early as 8,000 years ago. They point to a cat's jawbone dated 6000 B.C. discovered at an excavation site in southern Cyprus in 1983. Because this Mediterranean island has no native wild cats, it's believed the ancient kitty was brought there by human settlers.

DOMESTICATION

It's more generally accepted that cats were domesticated between 3,500 and 4,500 years ago in ancient Egypt. The first historical documents mentioning cats date from Egypt in 1668 B.C., and paintings of cats with collars tethered to chairs in homes are found in Theban tombs dating from about 1450 B.C.

More than likely, kitty domesticated herself because the arrangement was mutually beneficial. When humans turned from hunting game to cultivating crops, the harvest was a magnet to voracious vermin. The scurrying rodents that pilfered grain stores in turn drew wild cats to the feast. Humans soon learned that cats helped protect crops and food stores from the rodents, and so they encouraged the cats to stay.

Cats came to us to prey on the vermin that stored crops attracted.

The direct ancestry of the domestic house cat has long been argued. Today, most experts agree that the grand-daddy of all house cats is the African Wildcat, *Felis silvestris lybica.* Slightly bigger than modern house cats, this big yellow tabby roams the deserts of Africa, Syria, Egypt and parts of India, and matches the mummified remains of the domesticated cats of ancient Egypt.

The Glory Days

Cats became major symbols of power and virility in ancient Egypt, and were much admired for their mystical qualities. Some civilizations invented glorious superhuman beings that combined human and feline characteristics, like the famous lion-man figure of the Sphinx at Giza, found outside Cairo, Egypt.

Affection for cats reached its zenith when kitty was literally put on a pedestal. About 950 B.C., a city of the Nile delta called Bubastis worshiped a cat-headed goddess called Bast, or Pasht. She was the favorite of the sun-god, Ra, and was associated with happiness, pleasure, dancing and the warmth of the sun.

The smaller wildcats may have been brought into the temples to serve as surrogate deities because their size made them more manageable than lions or other big cats. Every move of the sacred temple cats was interpreted by the priests as a message from the goddess Bast.

Grace and Beauty

Feline grace was considered the epitome of beauty. The eyes of the African Wildcat are rimmed with a dark lining, and fine Egyptian ladies used cosmetics to outline their own eyes not only as protection from the sun, but perhaps to mimic the look of these cats. Egyptian law protected cats, and each one's death was greatly mourned. Cats were a jealously guarded treasure not

BLACK CATS

Throughout time, black cats have been both praised as being bearers of great luck and persecuted as harbingers of grave misfortune. The word *felis* is Roman for a good and auspicious omen, though the Romans also called cats *gatta*, meaning weasel.

In the Middle Ages, black cats were associated with sorcery, and many were killed in symbolic ceremonies.

Black cats are linked to fate in many countries. In America it's said that if a black cat crosses your path it's bad luck; in Ireland it foretells death in an epidemic; yet in England and Asia, it means you will have great luck.

Black cats were kept by sailors' wives to ensure their husbands' safety, and have starred in stories and poems by Edgar Allan Poe and William Butler Yeats. More recently, they have been pets to such celebrities as Jimmy Connors and Donna Mills.

allowed to leave the country. But some were stolen and smuggled out by covetous visitors. Kitty traveled from Egypt and was soon introduced around the world.

Out of Egypt

Cats first traveled from Egypt to India, and from there to China and Japan. Although writings by Confucius indicate he kept a pet cat in 500 B.C., cats were also treated as a delicacy there and eaten. But in Japan, cats were held in such high esteem that they guarded precious manuscripts in pagodas, and for several centuries ownership was restricted to members of the Japanese nobility.

It was considered good luck if a cat crossed your path, and it was believed that light-colored cats brought their owners silver while dark-colored cats brought them gold. So instrumental were cats in catching mice in silk factories that they're credited with saving the silk industry.

The next stop was Greece and Rome, where cats were kept along with ferrets to guard the grain. Some people, though, seemed to appreciate Kitty for more than her mousing abilities. Scientists studying the entombed city of Pompeii found a woman who died in the lava while holding her pet cat in her arms.

Throughout time, cats have been highly prized—and highly feared.

The Greek fablist Aesop included cats in a number of his works from the sixth century, B.C. Remember *The Cat and the Fox*, in which the cat "outsmarts" the sly fox himself? Or *The Cat and the Mice*, in which an old cat tries to deceive her prey but they don't take the bait? These stories were rooted in traits we associate with cats to this day: cleverness, quick thinking and secretiveness.

9

Cats were introduced into Northern Europe by the 10th century, probably by hitching rides on seafaring vessels. Crusaders who had traveled to the Middle East inadvertently brought back rats and house mice with them, and cats helped control these pests on the ships.

In early England, cats were quite rare and were highly prized as rat catchers. Laws of the day specified stiff fines for anyone who killed a cat.

THE FIRST CAT

There are a number of different legends that explain how cats made their entrance into the world. According to Hebrew folklore, Noah was concerned that rats might be a problem on the ark—eating all the provisions—and prayed to God for help. God responded by causing the lion, who was sleeping, to unleash a giant sneeze from which emerged a little cat.

In an Arabic legend, Noah's sons and daughters are worried about their safety on the ark because of the presence of the lion. Noah prayed to God for help and God afflicted the lion with a fever. But not too much later another dangerous creature emerged: the mouse. Again Noah prayed and this time God caused the lion to sneeze and the cat issued forth.

In a medieval legend the Devil plays a role in the creation of the cat. Trying to copy God and create a man, the evil Devil manages only to produce a small, pathetic, skinless animal—the cat. St. Peter felt sorry for the creature and gave it a fur coat, which is the cat's only valuable possession. (From *The Quintessential Cat*, by Roberta Altman. New York: Macmillan, 1994.)

To America

How did the domestic cat reach our shores? It had a transatlantic job to do: keep ships free of mice. And, probably too, keep the ship's passengers company. Though the North American Indians did not seem to have domestic cats, some archaeologists believe the cat was worshipped in Peru, in South America. When early settlers' colon-ies became rat-infested, the c   a   t was called on again and gained a permanent place in American homes.

Cats as Pagans

New religions often incorporate the symbols of established beliefs to attract a following. Consequently, the link of cats to pagan religions forged a bond with early Christianity, and, at first, cats were a positive symbol in the new order. The cat symbolized good, while the "devil" mouse exemplified evil. Kitty was often found in early pictures of the Holy Family, as a symbol of motherhood associated with the

Virgin Mary.

Later, when the church began to feel threatened by any association with paganism, the cat became a symbol and scapegoat for every evil imaginable.

In Europe, cats were killed in the name of religion throughout the Middle Ages, and by the 13th century, cats were irrevocably linked to witchcraft and persecuted unmercifully. When flea-infested rats carried the plague to Europe, there weren't enough rat-killing cats left to make a difference, and 75 million people died during the Byzantine Empire and the 14th century.

Popular Again

Kitty finally began clawing her way back into popularity by mid–17th century France. During the reign of Louis XV, keeping pampered felines became the rage for high-society ladies. The first

Cats moved in from the barn-yard to the parlor with the invention of kitty litter in the 1940s.

cat show was staged in St. Giles, Winchester, England, in 1598, but selective breeding wasn't popular until the mid–19th century.

A renewed interest and concern for pet cats stirred society's moral outrage against the cruelties inflicted upon animals. The world's first animal protection society was formed in England in 1824. The American Society for the Prevention of Cruelty to Animals was founded in 1866, followed ten years later by the American Humane Association.

Fancy Cats

In 1871, a cat show was held at London's Crystal Palace, and the English cat fancy was born ("fancy" is a term applied to people who get together primarily to show their cats, but also to breed them according to standards of perfection). Early cat shows had classes for some already established breeds—the Abysinnian, Manx and Royal Cat of Siam—as well as for shorthaired cats, longhaired cats and hybrid cats, heave cats and gelded cats. There was even a class for "Cats Belonging to Worming Men." The oldest and largest cat association in Great Britain is the Governing Council of the Cat Fancy, formed in 1910.

A cat show was held in Madison Square Garden in New York on May 8, 1895, leading to the creation of the cat fancy in this country. Though smaller shows for cats had been held in conjunction with poultry shows throughout the Northeast, the New York show was its own distinguished affair, despite sweltering temperatures that day.

Several cat clubs sprang up, and all had their enthusiasts. The most widely known today is the Cat Fanciers Association, started in 1906. There is also the American Cat Fanciers Association, The International Cat Association and three other smaller registry organizations. In 1945, there were only six breeds of cats on our shores; today there are over forty. Classes at shows range from those for the breeds to classes for kittens, altered cats and household cats.

MYTHS AND SUPERSTITIONS ABOUT CATS

- A cat has nine lives.

- Cats' eyes shine at night because they are casting out the light they gathered during the day.

- When a cat's whiskers droop, rain is coming.

- If you want to keep a cat from straying, put butter on its feet.

- If a cat sneezes near a bride on her wedding day she will have a happy marriage.

- A man who mistreats his cat will die in a storm.

- Stepping over a cat brings bad luck.

Down on the Farm

Through the years, cats continued to be prized as guardians of grain. In America, Kitty earned her keep by policing the haylofts and barnyards of farms, and running pest patrol in city warehouses. Canned cat food was introduced in the 1930s, but even fifty years ago most cats visited warm laps and firesides infrequently.

A 1947 innovation, Kitty Litter, changed the life-style of cats forever. Before, Kitty performed potty duty outside, and the rare indoor cat settled for a box of sand or ashes. The convenience of new litter products moved many cats from the barnyard into the parlor. When dry and semimoist cat foods appeared in the 1960s, cats were no longer kept strictly as mousers. Cats had become the pet of choice for the enlightened.

Despite a growing affection for them, little was known about cats. Cats, it was said, were independent little creatures who took care of themselves. Just thirty years ago, veterinarians were still treating cats the same as little dogs.

But soon, their growing popularity made industry sit up and take notice. New products not only catered to existing feline fans; they encouraged others to discover the wonderful world of cats. During the 1970s, scratching posts and creative litter pans designed to help outdoor cats transfer to an indoor lifestyle brought owners closer to their cats, enriching the lives of both.

The decade also brought a wealth of feline medical advances, and cats became a veterinary specialty when the American Association of Feline Practitioners was founded in the early 1970s. These advances made sharing our lives with cats even more rewarding.

The City Kitty

The 1980s brought increasing changes in social structures and lifestyles when people began, more and more, to live in cities and apartments. Cats were perceived to be convenience pets because they were just the right size for apartment living and didn't demand daily walks like dogs. Consequently, the late 1980s saw cats surpass dogs as the number-one pet of choice in the United States.

About the same time, researchers began studying the human–companion animal bond and discovered what cat lovers had known all along: Cats are good for you. Stroking a cat lowers blood pressure. A cat in the house buffers stress, which reduces stress-related illness and can even prolong life. Kitty took the news in stride and began making day-trips to hospital wards as a therapy cat. By 1994, the number of pet cats in the United States rose to 59.4 million.

Your kitten has traveled far to find a home in your welcoming arms. No longer the wild child of nature, cats retain an aura of mystery we humans find hard to resist. And although kittens seem angelic one moment and impish the next, today's cat is considered neither deity nor devil. Having crossed the threshold from barnyard to parlor, the cat has taken her rightful place as pampered pet. But more than that, your kitten will become a cherished friend—and a true member of the family.

> ## A CAT BY ANY OTHER NAME
>
> In English it's *cat*; in French, *chat*. The Germans call them *Katzen*, the Spanish and Syrians *gatos* and the Arabs *qitt*. The ancient Byzantine word was *katos*, the Latin *catus*. All are from *kadiz*, which was the word for cat in Nubia, an ancient Nile Valley kingdom that included southern Egypt.

By adopting your furry wonder, you've entered the enchanted world of cats. Open your eyes and your heart, and prepare for the smiles to come. Your magical journey together has just begun.

chapter 2

The
Physical
Kitten

Although every cat shares the same qualities and physical characteristics that define him as a cat, each feline is also unique. Kittens come in a variety of distinctive coat colors, patterns and hair lengths, and even their body shapes vary. Certain features are most apparent in purebred cats, but every cat, even the new kitten frisking about your feet, leans toward a certain feline "type."

The Outer Package

Non-pedigreed kitties are categorized by the length of their fur as either Domestic Shorthair (DSH) or Domestic Longhair (DLH) cats. Coat length runs the gamut from extremely short, satinlike fur, to luxurious flowing tresses. Some cats even have unusual wavy or crinkly "wire hair" coats.

The coat is composed of four types of hairs. The soft undercoat that keeps Kitty warm is called *down*. Middle-length hairs, called *awn hairs*, insulate and protect the skin, while the longest, thickest hairs are *guard hairs* making up the protective outer coat. The whiskers are wirelike *vibrissae* found mostly on the face but also on the back of the legs.

Coat Color

Coat color adds even more variety. Solid-color kittens are striking and range from black, dark gray (called blue), brown or light gray (called lilac) to red, cream or snow white. Bicolor patterns are two distinct solid colors, like the striking black and white "tuxedo cats."

PATTERNS AND COLORS

Did you know there are many terms to describe the colors and markings of your cat? Read this chapter to find out what they all mean.

Calico

Tabby

Pointed

Snow White

Tipping

Agouti

Tuxedo

Tortoiseshell and calico coloring appears only rarely in male cats, and when it does, usually he is sterile. A tortoiseshell kitten is black with red streaks or patches, and white cats with patches of red and black are called calico.

Some solid-color kittens sport shaded fur, which means the tip of each hair is darker or lighter than the rest of the hair. Tipping adds a sparkling or smoky shimmer to the coat. Agouti coloring looks like rabbit fur, where each individual hair is banded with various colors. Abyssinian cats have agouti coloring that ranges from fawn to deep red, brown, or even blue.

The Siamese cat is best known for his pointed pattern, in which his tail, legs, and muzzle are darker than his light-color body. Longhair cats like the Himalayan also may have dark points.

Tabby is not a breed of cat. The term describes the dark-on-light markings that occur in nearly every color.

The mackerel tabby sports a tiger-stripe pattern, while the classic tabby has a marbled look. In the spotted tabby, the kitten's body is covered with spots while tail and lower limbs are striped. Some cats even have interesting combinations of tabby patterns.

Your kitten's fur is a protective barrier between her body and the world.

Fur Function

Besides being beautiful, healthy fur is a protective barrier between your kitten's body and the environment. Well-groomed fur falls in smooth, loose-lying layers that insulate. During severe cold, saliva from grooming smooths the hair coat so that it becomes a more efficient insulator, helping to maintain body heat.

Perspiring is one way of lowering body temperature when overheated, and, like other mammals, cats have sweat glands. But only the specialized eccrine glands produce watery sweat like ours, and they're located on Kitty's paw pads. These sweat glands aren't particularly effective for heat loss. Instead, self-grooming helps the cat cool off.

By keeping his coat free of mats, the cat can elevate and "fluff" his fur, which opens the coat and allows air to pass between the hairs. This can either cool the skin or allow in extra heat. When very hot, cats also pant to cool themselves, but as much as a third of the

17

evaporative-cooling process occurs when the cat licks his skin and hair. Evaporation of saliva spread on the fur by grooming is an extremely effective means of keeping cool.

Self-grooming also helps the cat maintain healthy skin. Tugging at the hair coat stimulates sebaceous glands in the skin at the base of the individual hairs, which produce sebum. Sebum lubricates and waterproofs fur, and is spread by the cat's tongue when he grooms himself. Sebum also contains cholesterol, which is converted by sunlight into vitamin D. It is through washing that Kitty absorbs much of his nutritional requirement of vitamin D, which contributes to healthy bone and teeth, and aids calcium and phosphorus absorption and utilization.

Siamese cats like this kitten have the "foreign" body type.

Body Type

Most DSH and DLH have the *domestic* body type, an average-appearing yet muscular body. Persian cats typify the *cobby* body type, with a flattened face, round head and eyes, and short thick legs. The third general body type is the *foreign* model, which is a more lightly built, very slim cat with larger ears, slanted eyes and a longer, narrower muzzle, like the Siamese. Does your kitten tend toward the foreign or cobby body type? He may have Siamese or Persian in his background.

Even tails vary from cat to cat. Most DSH and DLH cats have long, supple tails. A kitten may be born with a short thick tail, a twisted puffy bunny tail, or no tail at all. Tailless breeds of cats include the Manx, the American Bobtail and the Japanese Bobtail. If your kitten is a tailless wonder, perhaps it's because of a tailless ancestor.

Boy or Girl?

A furry body may hide things you want to know. It's sometimes hard to tell whether you've adopted a boy or girl kitten. Lift your kitten's tail to determine gender. The position of a female's vulva and anus resembles a semicolon, while a male's furry behind looks more like an exclamation point. As your boy matures, his testicles will become more apparent.

A Feline Slinky

Despite distinctive coats, cats are very similar under the fur. Muscles holding the skeleton together give cats an incredible range of movement. Your kitten is so flexible he can pretzel his spine 180 degrees. That's because cats have five more vertebrae than people, with extras behind the shoulders. Seven cervical, thirteen thoracic, seven lumbar and three sacral vertebrae held together by muscles instead of ligaments make your kitten very muscular.

> ### AGE AND LIFESPAN
>
> How does a cat's age compare with a human's? When your cat's 1, he's 15 in human years; at 2, he's 25; and it slows down from there, averaging about an additional three years each during a cat's teens and twenties. Therefore, when your cat's 14, he's 72 human years old, and at the ripe age of 19, he's 87.
>
> Cats have been reported to live over thirty years—ancient in human years!

Shoulder blades placed on his sides allow your kitten to move his front legs in nearly every direction. His shoulder blades are attached to muscle rather than to a collarbone, which increases the cat's extreme elasticity.

Feet and Claws

If it seems your kitten "tippy-toes," you're right. Cats are digitigrade: They walk on their toes. This, combined with the unique shoulder blade placement, give Kitty a long, fluid stride.

Catch Kitty now while you can, because when he grows up, he'll run nearly thirty miles an hour. Tails are used for balance during high-speed turns and when exploring precarious heights. In fact, many domestic cats are exceptional jumpers and climbers who can jump five times their own height.

*Cats use their
paws to touch
things and see if
they're safe.*

Curved claws allow Kitty to climb as quickly as he runs on the ground. It's not so easy coming down, though, and cats often mew for help or shimmy backward down the tree.

Cat claws, made of keratin, grow from the last bone of each toe. Because they never stop growing, claws often need clipping just like human fingernails. Claws retract beneath the skin when Kitty is relaxed, and they extend when Kitty flexes his muscles, contracting the tendons and straightening the toes. Some cats even have extra toes, called *polydactylism.* If your kitten is a "mitten cat" with extra thumbs, he inherited them from his parents.

Although full of energy, your kitten needs frequent naps. Even adult cats typically sleep up to sixteen hours a day. But about seventy percent of rest is spent in light catnaps, during which Kitty remains aware of scents, sounds and the world around him.

Sense of Touch

One of the first sensations your kitten experienced was his mother's tongue washing and massaging his furry little body. Touch is a pleasurable sensation to cats, and is important both physically and emotionally. Petting your kitten not only lowers your own blood pressure; it does the same for the cat. Pleasurable touch promotes relaxation and reduces stress.

Tiny pressure-sensitive lumps are scattered over the cat's body, making the entire skin very touch-sensitive. Your kitten enjoys being stroked, but he can feel even indirect contact. A single hair being disturbed will trigger a response in the pressure point nearest that hair—and alert your kitten.

HOW WHISKERS WORK

Because stiff whiskers (*vibrissae*) are set much deeper in the skin than other hair, they are extremely sensitive and act like a kind of kitty antennae. Whiskers help protect the eyes, by triggering a blink reflex when something brushes them. Cat whiskers are also sensitive to air pressure and currents in relation to close objects, which helps Kitty judge distance.

The cat's whiskers act as "feelers," sensing whether he'll fit through a space.

When your kitten curiously sticks his head into a small opening, whiskers tell him whether he'll fit through the space. And in darkness, whiskers on his face and legs help him avoid danger.

Just as young children poke fingers and grab objects, cats use their paws to tap and prod things to see whether they're safe. The hairless bottoms of your kitten's feet, the paw pads and the tip of his nose are most sensitive to touch.

21

Cats love warmth and can bear temperatures as high as 125 degrees before registering discomfort. Your kitten may, in fact, seem insensitive to heat; some kitties suffer a singed tail without reacting. But the cat can tell slight differences of a degree or two simply by touching the object with his sensitive nose.

A KITTEN

He's nothing much but fur
And two round eyes of blue,
He has a giant purr
And a midget mew.

He darts and pats the air,
He tarts and cocks his ear,
When there is nothing there
For him to see and hear.

He runs around in rings,
But why we cannot tell
With sideways leaps he springs
At things invisible—

Then halfway through a leap
His startled eyeballs close,
And he drops off to sleep
With one paw on his nose.

Eleanor Farjeon

(From *The Quintessential Cat*, by Roberta Altman. New York: Macmillan, 1994.)

Sense of Taste

Taste isn't nearly as important to cats as smell, although the two senses are closely linked and register in the same area of the brain. Taste buds on the edges of the tongue and inside the mouth and lips detect sour, salt, sweet and bitter just like we do.

Down the center of the tongue are rows of hooked, backward-pointing projections called *papillae*. But newborns have only a rim of papillae around the edge of the tongue for grasping mother's nipple when they nurse.

The adult kitty tongue rasps food and is also used as a grooming tool and to collect liquids when Kitty drinks. The curled tongue becomes a kitty spoon for drinking; lapping cats typically swallow after every four or five laps.

Kittens have twenty-six baby teeth that are lost from twelve weeks to six months of age and are replaced by thirty adult teeth. But cats don't use teeth to chew. They turn their head to one side and use teeth to grasp and shear food into swallowable portions.

Sense of Smell

Aroma identifies life for our cats; without scent, the cat would be lost. Newborns use scent to find their mother, stake out a preferred nipple and return time after time to the same scent-marked place. From birth on, Kitty is led around by the nose.

The outside ridged pattern of your kitten's nose leather is unique, like a fingerprint. His nose is part of the upper respiratory tract and includes the nostrils (*nares*) and the interior nasal cavity that runs the length of the muzzle. Open spaces in the bone called *sinuses* connect to the nasal cavity.

The nasal cavity is enclosed by bone and cartilage, and is divided by a midline partition into two passages, one for each nostril, that open into the throat behind the soft palate. The partition, called the *nasal septum*, is a vertical plate made of bone and cartilage.

All your kitten's senses work together to keep her attuned to the world.

How Smell Works

A series of rolled, bony plates called *turbinates* are found inside the nasal cavity. The sense of smell originates with olfactory cells and nerves located in the *olfactory mucosa*, three to six square inches of thick, spongy membrane that covers the turbinates.

Despite a small head, cats have a much greater number of scent-analyzing cells than we. People have 5 to 20 million such cells, while your kitten has 67 million.

23

Odors enter the nose as fine airborne particles. Millions of tiny hairlike receptors extend from the olfactory cells into the thin layer of mucus that keeps the area moist. Odor particles are dissolved in the moisture, then make contact with the receptors. The dissolved odor particles stimulate olfactory nerves to signal the olfactory bulbs, which are directly linked to the brain. Once in the brain, exactly how smell is interpreted remains a mystery.

With over three times as many scent-analyzing cells as humans, cats have a much better sense of smell.

Your kitten's nose is not only a scenting organ, but also serves a protective function. The scroll-like strutures inside the nose increase the surface area that filters, warms and humidifies air. Glands throughout the nasal cavity form secretions that maintain moisture levels inside the nose. This protective coating traps bacteria and foreign bodies as a defense against infection.

EXTRA SCENT ORGANS

Cats also have extra scent organs, called Jacobson's organs, or *vomeronasal organs*. They specialize in scents that stimulate behavioral responses, especially sexual.

The vomeronasal organs are found in the mouth, between the hard palate and the nasal septum. Each organ is linked to *incisive ducts* that connect the oral cavity to the nasal cavity. The ducts open behind

Kitty's upper incisor teeth and permit air in the mouth to pass up into the nasal cavity.

To use the organs, Kitty traps scent particles on his tongue and then transfers them to the ducts behind his upper teeth. This behavior is known by the German term *flehmen*, roughly translated as "lip-curl." Such cats seem to grimace with mouth open and upper lip curled back, but what looks like repulsion actually indicates enthusiastic interest.

Flehmen is performed mainly by intact adult males, and it most often happens when they find the urine of a sexually receptive female kitty. Female cats also flehmen under certain conditions, and the behavior has been seen in kittens as young as two months.

Sense of Sight

Sight is probably the most important sense for cats. As hunters, cats rely on vision to find prey. In fact, cats have the largest eyes of any carnivore. If human eye-to-face ratio were the same as Kitty's, your eyes would be eight inches across!

Feline eye size and their location provide almost 280 degrees of three-dimensional sight. A cat's peripheral vision is sharper than his straight-ahead vision. Kitties are quite nearsighted, and they see motion more easily than stationary objects.

But cats see extremely well in the dark because they only need one-sixth the illumination level and use twice as much available light as people. Light reflects off the mirrorlike *tapetum lucidum*, a layer of cells at the back of the cat's eye, and is reflected back through the

---

THE EYES HAVE IT

A cat's eyes are truly unique. They are large and seated deep within the skull. This limits the amount the eyeball can move, but it allows for excellent peripheral vision, especially of moving objects. That is why the cat will dart its head to the side once it's detected movement from the side.

The vertical pupil responds quickly to changes in light, enlarging in the dark and closing to a slit in bright light. Cats are somewhat nearsighted; they can't see close-up objects too well. The pupils also close to a slit to help cats focus on nearby objects. Cats can see a limited range of colors.

All cat owners know that their kitty's eyes are hypnotic. They're the stuff of myth and legend, and even have a gemstone (Cat's-Eye) named after them. This stone has been used to protect people from witchcraft, make people invisible, and prevent women from getting pregnant when their husbands were away.

retina to augment vision. It's this reflected light that causes the eerie night shine we see in glowing feline eyes.

The colored area of your kitten's eyes is the iris, which is a figure-eight muscle that regulates how much light passes through. The iris is able to quickly open (dilate) the pupil into a circle when the light is low, or to shut it tight into a fine vertical slit in bright light. Light passes through the pupil and is focussed by the lens onto the retina at the back of the eye. Light-sensitive receptors on the surface of the retina transfer signals through the optic nerve to the brain, where the information is translated into vision.

Cats have the largest eyes of any carnivore.

Sense of Hearing

Cats respond better to high-pitched voices perhaps because they can't hear low pitches as well as people can. But cats, especially youngsters like your kitten, out-hear people in the higher ranges. This allows Kitty to detect high-pitched mouse squeaks of up to 60,000 cycles per second. People with the sharpest ears can hear only about 20,000 cycles per second.

In the ear, the furred portion you see, called the *pina*, can rotate 180 degrees and is used to funnel sound waves into the *auditory canal*. There, the fragile membrane of the *ear drum* resonates when struck by sound waves. The vibration is amplified by a complex system of tiny bones and fluid-filled tubes of the inner ear. Then, signals are transmitted to the brain, where they are interpreted as sound.

Balancing Act

The *vestibular apparatus* of the inner ear also gives your kitten his uncanny sense of balance. Coupled with vision and the elastic strength of his spine, Kitty's innate equilibrium allows him to become an acrobat during falls. He twists and turns in midair to land nearly always on his feet.

For the righting mechanism to work properly, however, cats must be awake, and they must have enough distance in which to turn. Falls from very short heights, like from a child's arms, may not give Kitty enough time to turn. And falls from heights that are too great can result in broken legs and a split jaw when Kitty hits the ground, even if he makes a perfect four-foot landing.

Cats' ears are designed to pick up high-pitched noises—like the squeak of a mouse.

Your Happy, Healthy Kitten

Your Kitten's Name _____

Where Your Kitten Came From _____
_____

Your Kitten's Birthday _____

Your Kitten's Favorite Toys _____
_____

Your Kitten's Favorite Sleeping Spot _____
_____

Your Kitten's Veterinarian

    Name _____

    Address _____

    Phone Number_____

    Emergency Number_____

Your Kitten's Health

    Vaccines

    type _____ date given _____

    type _____ date given _____

    type _____ date given _____

    type _____ date given _____

Your Kitten's Coat Color _____

Your Kitten's Eye Color_____

Your Kitten's Body Type _____

chapter 3

Indoor/Outdoor Concerns

Should cats be allowed outside? Or should they be exclusively indoor pets? Ask any five cat lovers, and you'll get five opinions on this emotional issue. For your kitten's sake, you must seriously consider the questions raised by this passionate debate.

Exclusively indoor cats lead a protected, sheltered life. These cats leave their homes only in a carrier or when taken for a walk on a leash. Indoor/outdoor cats often live inside but are allowed access to outdoor delights. Exclusively outdoor cats spend all their time outside.

Clearly, each choice offers dramatic lifestyle differences for both you as your kitten's caretaker and for the kitten herself. Individuals on each side of the figurative fence consider themselves responsible, caring cat lovers and argue they've made the best choice for their cat. Exactly what are the arguments? And which is the best choice for your kitten?

Outdoor Delights

Today, few pet cats are called upon to earn their keep policing mouse and rat populations. But many cat lovers and some experts believe that outdoor cats enjoy

Outdoor cats may enjoy a more natural life—but are the risks worth it?

a more natural lifestyle.

Where else can a cat run and jump, climb trees, sniff and chase bugs and other prey and satisfy her feline curiosity so well? The cat's social behavior seems tailored to life in spacious areas; cats in crowded indoor environments may develop destructive behaviors.

Felines kept exclusively indoors can become bored if there's not enough stimulation to keep their kitty brains occupied—or enough exercise to release their energy. In some instances, frustrated indoor cats may develop stress-related health conditions.

Changing the litter box is the least appealing aspect of keeping a cat, and the convenience of Kitty making her toilet outdoors is an agreeable notion to owners. There are also innumerable outdoor scratching opportunities that seem designed with kitty claws in mind, so an outdoor lifestyle may reduce the damage done to your furniture.

Proponents of the outdoor lifestyle believe it is better for Kitty to enjoy life to the fullest, even if her life is shortened by the consequences of outdoor living.

Outdoor Risks

It is a myth that cats easily return to a wild existence and are able to care for themselves. Domestication has suppressed or even silenced many of the feral skills necessary for survival. Making a pet fend for herself is like abandoning a three-year-old child; she may survive a short time but eventually will succumb to a cruel death.

In fact, the typical outdoor cat's life span is short compared to that of exclusively indoor cats, who often live into their late teens and beyond. Quite simply, life on the outside poses much greater risks for lethal disease and injury.

Your kitten loves warm places to snooze, and many outdoor cats are attracted to a perch beneath the hood of a car. The poor cat caught by the fan or belt when the engine starts is permanently crippled, if not killed.

It only takes a second for a kitten to escape from your house or the yard.

Even savvy cats get into trouble. It takes only one mistake. Kitty can accidentally hitchhike in a strange vehicle and find herself far from home. Curious cats become trapped in outbuildings where their cries cannot be heard, or they fall into swimming pools and drown.

Outdoor Enemies

But the number-one killer and crippler of outdoor cats is car accidents. Even usually attentive cats lose their concentration and dash into oncoming traffic when being chased by a dog, pursuing prey, or distracted by other kitty delights.

Fights with other outdoor cats lead to dangerous bite and scratch wounds that can easily become infected. Even worse, viral diseases like rabies and feline leukemia are spread by contact with infected animals or contaminated environments. Remember, vaccinations cannot provide 100 percent protection, and reducing exposure is an important part of prevention.

The free-roaming cat is a magnet for parasites like

The outside world is full of kitty dangers, from chemicals to cars to intolerant neighbors.

fleas, ticks, mosquitoes and other buggy freeloaders, which are deposited in your yard and house when Kitty comes home. Found in grass, soil, rodents and other kitty hors d'oeuvres, parasites often transmit or cause dangerous disorders like tapeworms, anemia and heartworm disease.

Cats can be poisoned simply by grooming themselves after walking across treated lawns. And should Kitty manage to catch that mouse, she may ingest poison the rodent has already eaten.

Many parts of the country harbor dangerous predators like coyotes, eagles, alligators and great horned owls, who consider your kitten a tasty snack. Neighborhood dogs may not look kindly upon the free-roaming cat: not every kitty makes it up a tree unscathed. Cats who trespass in other yards and dig in gardens fuel the ire of otherwise-tolerant neighbors. Some unenlightened humans actually dislike cats, while others protest kitty paw prints on their clean cars. Bird watchers become particularly irate if a neighbor cat stakes out their bird feeder. Some people may be tempted to retaliate.

Knowing this, is it worth acquiring extra gray hairs each time your furry wonder wanders out of sight? Can you make your kitten comfortable with your choice? Is there a way to abide by your convictions and satisfy Kitty's emotional needs, yet keep her safe?

Examine the Choices

As a responsible caretaker, evaluate the outdoor risks in your particular area before making a choice. Do you live in an apartment in New York City, or in a farmhouse with a private road far out in the country? How close are your neighbors, and what pets do they have that your kitten might encounter? What wildlife might be tempted to snack on your cat? If your kitten has long fur, will you have the extra time needed to untangle and groom debris from her coat? And what about parasite control?

Before opening the door to your kitten, consider this: Once Kitty has become accustomed to an outside lifestyle, it's difficult (but not impossible) for her to be happy as an exclusively indoor pet. A kitten who has been kept inside since birth won't miss what she's never known.

In fact, cats sleep more than half the day away, and fifty percent of their awake time is spent grooming. The rest of their day is spent eating and drinking, taking care of "potty duty," or meditating, which they're perfectly content to perform indoors.

Exercise fills only a small part of Kitty's day, but is still extremely important to both her physical and mental well-being. This need can be met for exclusively indoor cats quite easily.

Bringing the Outdoors In

Exactly what is it that makes a cat yearn for the great

outdoors? Cats are sensory creatures who delight in smells, sounds, tastes and sights; even the sun feels good, and a doze in a puddle of sunshine charms the most finicky cat. Cats also need to exercise both their bodies and their minds. To keep the indoor cat happy and healthy, satisfy her craving for sensory stimulation: bring the outdoors in.

Your kitten is safest exploring the great outdoors under your supervision.

Cats often nibble grass and other vegetation when outside. Most feline nutritionists believe small amounts add beneficial dietary fiber or vitamins; more to the point, some cats dearly love veggies. Planting kits with oat grass seeds or catnip are available at pet supply stores to create indoor grazing opportunities.

Windows are tops with cats who use them as sunning perches or lookout posts to watch the world go by. Several kinds of window perches are available that attach to the sill and give Kitty more room to lounge. The best is a sturdy model that takes the weight of a cat (or two) and won't wobble when the cat turns it into a landing or launching pad.

How About a Friend

Adding a second cat or even a dog may keep your indoor kitten well occupied. A bird, rodent, reptile or even an aquarium of fish may please the voyeuristic cat.

Of course, extreme care must be taken that small pets are safe from the cat by ensuring cages are secure and aquarium covers are tight. Also, some birds dislike being viewed by a hungry-looking feline, and the emotional stress caused to the bird may outweigh the benefits gained by the cat.

Many indoor cats enjoy vicarious outdoor living by

viewing feline videos. Available through mail order or in pet supply stores, they are designed to bring the cat's favorite outdoor activities into the safety of his living room. They feature fluttering, chirping birds; swimming fish; and the antics of squirrels, lizards, rats, cats, bugs, butterflies and other inhabitants of the animal kingdom. Not all cats react to videos, but those

Kittens love to climb into all sorts of things.

who do enjoy hours of whisker- and tail-twitching satisfaction. (See chapter 12 for some suggestions.)

Scratching Posts and Other Diversions

Scratching is as natural to your kitten as touching and poking objects is to a human child. Outdoor cats scratch rough, stable objects like trees, and your indoor kitten needs the same scratching opportunities to stay happy. (See chapter 4 for more information.)

Feline playgrounds are designed to keep the bored cat interested and out of trouble. Cats love to play hide and seek, and designs that incorporate small openings and multilevel perches are ideal. Vertical designs take up only a small corner of the room while giving your kitten near-ceiling height to climb, claw, perch and hide. If you have carpentry skills, create your own kitty habitat. Pet supply stores offer the ultimate in cat furniture pleasure.

Making the Outdoors Safe

35

If you'd like your kitten to safely experience the out-doors up close and personal, consider leash training. Chapter 9 outlines ways to introduce the concept. But never tie or stake Kitty outside, because that leaves her at the mercy of other animals. Cats tend to get tangled easily and can injure themselves so quickly you may not have time to intervene.

Outdoor enclosures are another alternative. Designs vary from simple to elaborate and include everything from do-it-yourself modification of existing porches,

With a heavy tree trunk inside an enclosed outdoor area, your kitten can make believe she's in the wild.

decks and patios, to installation of modular cat houses and custom fencing. Appropriate furnishings like scratching objects and kitty playgrounds add to the fun.

Standard chain-length fence used for dog runs and kennels is adaptable for cat-approved outdoor enclo-sures. When designing for cats, chain length should be smaller (13-gauge, one-inch squares) so that Kitty can't stick her head through the fence and be injured. To keep Kitty from climbing out, covered runs are necessary, and they should be shaded to shield your cat from direct sunlight.

There are also commercial cat enclosures available that use contour-molded vinyl frames, hinges and latches that won't rust; and small units can be folded and moved from place to place. Cat condos are avail-able with lounging shelves, floor panels, dividers and even casters for easy mobility.

Creating a Sanctuary

Perhaps you'd prefer fencing the entire backyard to create a cat sanctuary. Before you begin, remember that some cats are expert climbers and their exploration won't be stopped by a fence. Even nonclimbing felines can be at risk if strange cats or dogs come after them. You may wish to consider a fence system that is accentuated by a netting barrier to keep intruders out. Check out cat magazines or your local pet store for possibilities.

How does your kitten get from the house to her outdoor haven? If the enclosure is on a porch, deck or similarly enclosed structure, simply propping open a door or window may be sufficient; outdoor enclosures can also be positioned near a window for convenience. But leaving a door or window open may not be feasible, since it allows bugs in and air conditioning out.

A variety of pet doors are available that let cats be their own doormen. From simple flaps to electronically controlled portholes, there's a model and price to suit each cat and owner. Cat doors can be installed in walls, doors, screens or windows, and many have lock-out options to keep the cat inside when necessary.

> ## WHAT EVIL LURKS . . .
>
> Before your kitten gets too used to living the indoor/outdoor life, consider the dangers to which she'll be exposed in the "natural" world:
>
> cars and other traffic
>
> parasites (ticks, fleas, worms)
>
> other cats
>
> dogs
>
> wildlife (including rabid animals)
>
> toxic chemicals
>
> unsympathetic neighbors
>
> This doesn't mean your kitten can never go outside. You can build or buy a variety of enclosures or teach your kitten to walk in a harness on leash, then the two of you can explore together.

In the best of all possible worlds, cats could safely climb trees, cross busy highways in pursuit of grasshoppers, and trespass in the neighbor's yard with impunity. But as long as there are viruses, parasites, big dogs and bigger cars, the outside cat will remain at risk, and concerned cat owners will continue the debate.

Responsible cat lovers on both sides of the fence must offer the best cat-safe options available. Make informed decisions not only to satisfy your new kitten but also to give yourself peace of mind.

Living

with Your

part two

Kitten

chapter 4

Bringing Your
Kitten
Home

Nothing beats a kitten for fun. But the feline "wonder years" can also be the most frustrating and dangerous time in your kitten's life. Don't let Kitty's innocent face fool you. Behind those twinkling bright eyes is a mind brimful of curiosity, and the boundless energy to try and satisfy it. Kittens have a way of turning the most innocuous situation into a disaster. Whether you survive with your sanity intact—and whether your kitten survives at all—can depend on your kitten-proofing your home.

Kitten-Proofing the House

Kitten-proofing is done to make the house safe so that Kitty doesn't hurt himself. It also prevents him from laying waste to your house so that you don't yearn to retaliate.

First, try to think like a cat. Invest in knee pads, get down on all fours, and tour your house at kitten level. But jumping and climbing kittens rarely stop at floor level, so you also need to kitten-proof the heights.

Despite evidence to the contrary, kittens do not have hands. Instead, they use patting paws to explore their world, and they stick their tiny noses into everything. Anything left within reach is fair game, so place anything breakable out of feline range. The more intelligent the kitten, the more ways he'll find to get into trouble.

TOXIC HOUSEPLANTS

Protect your kitten from houseplants . . . and vice versa. To a kitten, a large floor plant is an exotic jungle gym to scale, while a pot of soil is an invitation to furry excavators.

Kittens are boundless explorers, meaning anything they can get to is fair game.

Chewing houseplants like dieffenbachia, philodendron, pothos and English ivy can cause toxic reactions. Kitty may even lick off the poison when he grooms his claws after shredding the plant. Keep plants out of your kitten's reach by hanging them or placing them on shelves. Choose nontoxic plants like the jade plant, the prayer plant, the begonia, donkey tail, coleus or piggyback.

SECURING CORDS

Kittens don't tend to chew as much as puppies, but they do play-attack and bite nearly everything. Electric cords can be particularly tempting, and bitten cords can result in severe burns or even death. Get rid of as many electrical cords as possible, and check remaining wires regularly for signs of chewing. Tape cords to the floor to keep them from moving (and reduce Kitty's temptation to bat and bite them).

TRASH AND OTHER ITEMS

Keep garbage away from your kitten. Although cats are generally more fastidious than their canine counterparts, the smell of scraps may tempt Kitty to scrounge. Your kitten might be poisoned by eating potato eyes or chocolate, or she might end up with an upset stomach that results in a predictable mess. Securely fasten lids on trash containers, or store them under the sink or in the garage where the kitten can't reach them. Beware

Unsupervised games can turn into accidents.

leaving sharp knives, food processor blades or other utensils out on counters where Kitty might try to lick them clean—and cut her tongue.

Like children, kittens have a tendency to swallow small nonfood items like coins, pins, erasers and paper clips. Anything left out is fair game for the cat. Carefully cap all medications, and put them away. Pills are fun to bat around the floor, but if swallowed can be poisonous. *Aspirin and Tylenol are deadly to cats!*

DECORATION DISASTERS

Christmas is an enchanting yet dangerous time of year for kittens. The tree seems meant for climbing, and the blinking lights and swinging ornaments tempt the most stoic kitty to indulge. But broken ornaments, extra electric cords, metal hooks or tinsel, sprayed lead-base "snow" and tree needles all pose dangers. Avoid placing decorations on the bottom branches, be sure the tree is securely anchored, avoid tinsel, and use ribbon to hang nonbreakable ornaments.

TOYS AND STRINGS

Carefully inspect cat toys, and remove small eyes or tails that come loose and may be swallowed. Put away sewing baskets and tackle boxes. Kittens love to play with thread, string and yarn, but unsupervised games can lead to accidental strangulation, swallowed needles, cuts from fishing line or embedded fish hooks. Cats can swallow several yards of ribbon or string, which will require surgical removal. Tie up curtain cords out of kitten reach, or purchase breakaway cords. The standard double cords on window blinds can hang and strangle a kitten.

HIDING PLACES

Kittens and adult cats delight in cubbyholes in which to sleep. Always check cupboards and dresser drawers

Swinging ornaments tempt the most stoic kitty to indulge.

before shutting them, to be sure your kitten isn't hiding inside. Keep appliances closed. Kitty may think he's found the perfect warm hidy-hole to sleep—until the appliance is turned on. It may sound funny at first, but kittens die every day by being accidentally shut inside a dishwasher, washing machine, clothes dryer or stove.

FIRE

Fire will cause either fear or fascination in your kitten, and patting paws will get burned if he tries to catch the flame. Cats like warm places to sleep but may get singed when allowed unsupervised access to hot stove burners, irons or lit fireplaces.

Protect your sanity, and your new kitten's life, by running interference for the little guy and clearing lethal booby traps out of your house. Then sit back, relax and treasure the antics of the furry wonder who now shares your life. Kittenhood doesn't last forever, but kitten-proofing your home will ensure that the memories you make today will be happy ones. And happy kitty memories are oh-so-sweet, sweet enough to last a lifetime.

POISONOUS PLANTS

The following house and outdoor plants contain substances that are poisonous to cats. If chewed or ingested, these plants can cause symptoms from vomitting and diarrhea to rapid hearbeat, kidney problems, even death.

Chrysanthemum

Daffodil

Larkspur

Poinsettia

Jack-in-the-Pulpit

Bird of Paradise

Ivy

Skunk Cabbage

Elephant Ears

Azalea

Rhubarb

Marijuana

Nutmeg

Black Locust

Food and Water Dishes

Every kitten should have his own set of dishes. A variety of styles are available at most pet supply outlets, or even grocery stores. Your kitten probably won't care whether his bowls are plain or elaborate, but a number of cute styles are available to tickle any pet lover's fancy.

A minimum of two bowls is needed. One holds water, while the second is for food. Some owners settle for one dish for water, then use disposable paper plates for each kitty meal.

The perfect cat dish is heavy enough that Kitty won't have to "follow" it all over the room as he eats, and it is balanced so that it won't tip over. Shallow, wide bowls that have plenty of whisker room get feline raves. Cats don't like scrunching their whiskers or getting themselves dirty by diving head first into a deep bowl. Be sure to buy bowls that will please your kitten when he's adult size.

Food dishes must be easy to wash in order to remove odors that might offend delicate cat noses. Plastic dishes are hard to get clean, and some cats may have allergic reactions to them. Stainless steel dishes won't chip, crack or break; are easy to clean; and are dishwasher-safe, but they may be too lightweight. Ceramic or glass dishes are much better—and answer the needs of most cats.

A glass or ceramic bowl is good for kitty— and easy for you to clean.

The Litter Box

What goes in one end of the kitten as food and water must be dealt with at the other end. Standard kitten equipment includes a litter box, a slotted scoop and litter.

Kitty's bathroom facilities should be large enough for the cat to turn around easily, but not so large he can't see over the sides. Pans should be deep enough to hold at least two inches of litter for digging, but not be so shallow that he tosses litter onto the floor. Adult cats should have no trouble stepping into the box. Very young kittens may need to be helped into the box until they "grow" into the facilities.

Most commercial litter pans are about 5 x 12 x 18 inches and are made of easily cleaned plastic. These are generally fine for kittens. If your kitten grows into a monster cat, or if you have two cats who agree to share, larger pans are available. As with food bowls, all kinds of colors and styles are available in pet stores and mail-order catalogues. Covered models reduce the litter that enthusiastic diggers fling out of the box, and they also offer Kitty some privacy.

TYPES OF LITTER

The most popular litter today is clay-based granules that feel good to digging cat feet, absorb moisture and odor, and have a minimum of dust or tracking. Many brands are available, and new ones appear every day.

"Scoopable" litters are extremely convenient, because liquid waste congeals into firm balls that can be lifted out of the pan to prolong the life of the rest of the litter. Some litters can be flushed, which also makes them convenient.

Other litters are made of recycled paper, wheat, cedar shavings and other biodegradable products. What works for one cat may not appeal to another. When choosing a litter, remember that cats prefer sandy, soil-like textures with no perfumes or dust.

Cats like rough surfaces on which to climb and claw.

Slotted litter scoops lift waste from the soiled box but allow clean litter to sift back inside. Commercial scoops are available, but any slotted spoon or spatula will work. If your litter isn't flushable or your septic system can't handle litter, keep a covered wastebasket or diaper pail handy to deposit Kitty's offerings. A whisk broom or hand vacuum is helpful to clean up tracked litter.

Spray deodorants may make you feel better, but they will scare your kitten and offend his scent sense, too. The best way to handle litter box odor is to keep the box clean.

For Your Kitten's Comfort

Felines spend much of their lives sleeping, and they're most comfortable on a warm, cozy surface. There are a variety of **cat beds** on the market, available in numerous sizes, shapes and colors. Experiment with those if you like, or make your own soft spot for your kitten. This can be as simple as a special blanket in kitty's favorite spots, wherever that may be—a special chair, a windowsill, the top of the clothes dryer or your bed. Washable blankets are best. Your kitten will let you know which fabrics she prefers.

Because cats relish the view from the windowsill, you may want to construct a special **perch** for a particularly favored window. The perch could be small or large, depending on how you want to design it—anything from a carpet-lined plank to curl up on to a climbing station with a view. Pet supply stores and catalogs will give you ideas.

For Your Kitten's Fun

You'll want to have a supply of **toys** for your kitten to keep her occupied—and you'll want to share this activity with her. With their fascination for moving objects, it's not hard to come up with simple, fun toys. An all-time favorite is the kitty fishing rod. From a two- or three-foot pole, attach a foot-long length of twine or strong string to which you've tied a large feather or a stuffed sock or a small ball. From the comfort of your chair you can play "fish" with your kitten, who will spend hours chasing and catching the object at the end of the pole.

A look through any pet supply store or catalog will supply you with a slew of ideas for toys you can buy or make. Cats love to explore, so cardboard boxes with cutaway entrances make great toys. There are fabric-lined tubes you can buy for your kitty to run through, as well as a host of squeaky, fleecy and bouncy toys.

Another favorite amusement is **catnip**. The plant itself is a member of the mint family, and it's the chemical it contains that gets kitties going. That chemical is nepetalactone; it triggers something in the scent glands that has a euphoric effect on cats. They respond by licking, chewing or rubbing the plant or a catnip-filled toy. Like mint, catnip is fairly easy to grow, and you can plant your own crop from which to pick and dry leaves. Or you can buy dried catnip and already-made toys in pet supply stores.

Scratching Posts

Cats scratch. Period. There is no way to stop it, and even declawed cats go through the motions. Therefore, a proper scratching object is a necessity.

Because many owners don't understand why the cat scratches, they choose a scratching object Kitty refuses to use. Cat claws, like human fingernails, grow constantly. Dragging claws through rough fabric like upholstery or carpet helps remove the outer sheath and makes room for new growth. It's also great exercise that simply feels good, and cats often scratch to express happiness or to mark territory.

Your kitten basically is looking for a nail file that's tall enough or long enough to give his muscles a good, stretching workout. The scratching object must be sturdy and stable enough that a full kitty assault won't knock it over.

Many carpet-covered scratching posts are available that match any decor, but don't let simple looks sway you. If the scratching object doesn't meet Kitty's criteria, he'll find something that does, like the living room sofa, the plaster wall or a chair leg.

WHAT TO LOOK FOR

The best commercial scratching posts have a rough cover that files Kitty's nails; sisal, tree bark or very dense carpet work well. Choose a post that your kitten won't outgrow. Make sure it doesn't slide around or tip over when he's using it, or Kitty may never go near the post again. Scratching posts are available in pet supply stores, or through mail order.

Some cats relish homemade scratching objects. A piece of cordwood from the fireplace is the simplest way to go. For the ambitious, use carpet remnants and mount them *wrong side out* on a plywood sheet or wooden post. Any of these can be secured against the wall or on a wooden base, or simply left flat on the floor for horizontal scratchers.

The Traveling Cat

Even exclusively indoor cats must occasionally make a trip to the groomer or veterinarian. A variety of versatile, safe cat carriers is available, and a carrier should always be used even when Kitty is traveling short distances.

Your kitten will travel with you happily if you get her used to it gradually.

Some cats get so upset while traveling that they may have accidents, and confining them to a carrier makes cleanups much easier. More importantly, your distraught kitten could slip through your arms on the way to the car and become lost. Kittens and cats allowed to roam in a moving car can cause injury to themselves or others by blocking the view or getting under the driver's feet.

The carrier you choose should be large enough for the adult cat to turn around in, yet not so large that Kitty rattles about like salt in a shaker. Cats prefer quarters that make them feel more secure. The hard plastic airline-approved carriers are very safe and readily available. Space-capsule-type carriers or soft-sided duffle-type bags with zippers are also popular. Inexpensive cardboard carriers are usually available at pet stores or veterinarians. Confining Kitty to a cat carrier while traveling is safest for all concerned. If possible, secure the carrier with a seatbelt.

Grooming Supplies

Although cats have a well-deserved reputation as fastidious creatures, kittens do get grubby from time to time. Longhair cats absolutely cannot stay clean on their own; they need your help keeping all that fur in shape. Unless you prefer to shave the cat, regular combing is essential for longhair kitties to keep them from matting. Brushing and combing benefits all cats by reducing the amount of hair they shed—or swallow and spit up as hairballs.

A soft-bristle brush may be all that's necessary for a shorthair kitten. A rubber curry brush will help remove shed fur, and a fine-tooth flea comb is handy when a bath won't do.

For longhair cats, groomers recommend a stainless steel comb that has very wide teeth on one end and medium to narrow teeth on the other. Sometimes called a "greyhound comb" or "Belgian flip comb," one with a Teflon coating will help prevent Kitty's hair from being pulled and will also reduce static electricity. The longer and thicker your kitten's hair, the wider-toothed the comb should be. A natural or wire-bristled "slicker" brush helps finish long coats.

Keeping your kitten's nails trimmed will knock those razor points off, protect your ankles, and even reduce

---

GROOMING SUPPLIES

There are basic grooming tools all cat owners should have. Types of brushes vary depending on whether your cat has short hair (SH) or long hair (LH). Basic tools include:

soft-bristle brush (SH)

natural or wire slicker brush (LH)

rubber curry brush (SH)

stainless steel wide-tooth comb (LH)

fine-tooth flea comb

cat nail clippers

flea shampoo

baby oil

cotton balls

commercial ear-cleaning solution

gauze pads

saline solution

some of her urge to scratch. As long as Kitty is tiny, human nail trimmers will suffice. Invest in commercial cat nail clippers for older kittens and adults. Guillotine-type or scissor-action styles are available. (For more on grooming, see chapter 6.)

Bathing Supplies

You'll also need bathing supplies. Yes, cats can and do tolerate bathing far better than most people realize. Some kitties actually enjoy the experience. By starting your kitten early, she won't know she's "supposed" to hate water.

First, you'll need a mild shampoo for basic cleaning. People shampoo is too harsh and can cause skin irritation, and dishwashing detergent can be toxic, so stick to pet products labeled safe for kittens. Some of the best cat-cleaning products mimic the pH of the kitten's skin and are available at pet supply outlets or your veterinarian's office. Static electricity in the fur of longhair kittens can make them look like they stuck their tail in an electric socket, and coat conditioners may help.

If fleas are a problem, shampoos with pyrethrin insecticides are considered the safest. Just be sure any product you choose is labeled for kittens, and carefully follow directions. Never mix flea products, or you could turn otherwise safe shampoos into deadly concoctions.

Finally, kitten grooming supplies should include baby oil, cotton balls, cotton swabs, a commercial ear-cleaning solution, gauze pads and saline solution. These will help you keep your kitten's eyes, ears and teeth as clean as her fluffy fur. (For more on bathing, see chapter 6.)

Collaring Kitty

All cats, even those kept exclusively indoors, should wear a collar with identification. It takes just a moment for your new kitten to slip out the door, and tags can help ensure his safe return if he becomes lost.

But the cat's delicate neck can be easily injured by ill-fitting or poorly designed collars. Collars that catch on objects can hang and strangle the cat. Choose a collar designed with elastic inserts that stretch to release tangled cats. Collars should fit snugly, with room for two fingers to fit easily underneath. Sometimes the size of a cat's neck isn't much different than the size of his head, so even a properly fitting collar may tend to slide off.

Never, ever attach the leash to a cat's collar. A hysterical cat can leap and quite literally break his neck. A cagey cat may simply turn and back away, pull the collar off, and disappear. A harness and leash are the proper cat-walking equipment.

The preferred harness for cats is either a lightweight figure-H or figure-eight halter. One strap goes around the cat's neck, while the other wraps about his body behind the forelegs. The leash should be lightweight cloth, nylon or leather, no longer than six feet. The leash is attached to a metal ring in the harness above the cat's shoulders.

KITTY'S BASIC NEEDS

These are the things all kittens need, and you're better off getting them *before* your kitten comes home, so you're prepared.

food dish

water dish

cat carrier

collar

identification tag

grooming tools

litter tray

bed

first aid kit

harness and leash

Bedtime

Your kitten should have a safe place to which he can retire and not be disturbed. Countless designer cat beds are available, from fleece-lined teepees and tunnels to nestlike cat lounges or even kitty hammocks.

But a soft, cuddly blanket inside his cat carrier may just as easily tickle your kitten's fancy. Often, the kitten chooses where he wants to sleep. You may need to gently dissuade him if you don't want to share your pillow.

chapter 5

Feeding
Your
Kitten

Whether your kitten is destined to be a finicky feline or a gourmet glutton, mealtimes will be major events in her life. Kittens depend on good nutrition not only to fuel their daily play, but to ensure they grow up healthy and stay that way.

Nutritional Needs

Nutrients are the substances in food that provide nourishment. Cats require a combination of six different

classes of nutrients for good health: water, protein, carbohydrates, lipids (fats), minerals and vitamins.

PROTEIN

Protein is composed of many amino acids needed for good feline health. Protein provides energy and builds healthy skin, fur, nails, ligaments, cartilage and tendons. Although your kitten's body can synthesize some amino acids, those that can't be made by the body—the *essential amino acids*—must be acquired through the diet. Some nutrients can be obtained only in meat; for instance, without the essential amino acid *taurine* found in meat protein, cats can develop heart disease or go blind.

In fact, cats require four times more protein than dogs do; they also need more dietary fats than dogs do, and some must come from animal protein (that's why your kitten should not be fed dog food).

Some of the nutrients cats need can only be obtained from meat.

Cats absolutely cannot survive on vegetarian diets; they must have animal protein in their daily ration. But meat alone doesn't contain the right balance of nutrients that a kitten needs. In the wild, cats eat the entire mouse and gain vitamins and minerals from the organs, as well as vegetable nutrients from the mouse's last meal. In today's foods, cats get protein from meats, fish, poultry and eggs. A portion of the cat's diet can come from vegetable proteins and carbohydrates.

CARBOHYDRATES

Carbohydrates supply energy. They also help the central nervous system and the gastrointestinal tract function. Carbohydrates are obtained from sugars and starches like some vegetables and grains.

FATS

Fat makes food taste good, and it's a vital nutrient despite the negative associations it has for us. Fat supplies fuel for energy and helps transport vitamins. Fat deposits protect the body from heat loss.

VITAMINS AND MINERALS

Vitamins contribute to numerous bodily functions, and too much or too little of a vitamin can have a major effect on your cat's health. Vitamins come in two forms: fat soluble and water soluble. Fat-soluble vitamins—like A, D, E and K—are stored in fat and not passed through the body, while water-soluble vitamins like C and the B-complex vitamins are. It's especially important that your cat doesn't get too many fat-soluble vitamins. For this reason, supplementing a premium commercial cat food is not suggested. Any conditions you suspect are related to a vitamin deficiency should be discussed with your veterinarian.

Minerals contribute to strong bones and teeth. Calcium and phosphorous are two commonly known minerals. Did you know your kitty also needs copper, zinc, manganese, iodine, iron and potassium, to name a few other minerals?

> ### GRASS FOR YOUR CAT
>
> Cats crave the nutrients in grass, and wheat grass is especially beneficial for your feline. You can grow a patch of wheat grass at home and make it available to your cat. Buy organic hard wheat berries at a health food store. You'll need about one tablespoon per crop. Soak the wheat berries overnight in water, then drain and allow the berries to dry on a piece of paper towel. In a ceramic bowl, place approximately one inch of potting soil and plant the berries in it. Spray the soil with water, then cover the layer of wheat berry seeds with one-quarter inch of peat moss or more soil. Place in a bright area. Keep moist, and avoid overwatering or the crop will get moldy. The grass should be ready for your cat in a week or ten days.

If you think kitty nutrition sounds complicated, you're right. That's why feline nutritionists recommend feeding a commercially prepared food to your kitten. The principal ingredients of cat foods are meat, poultry, seafood, feed grains like corn or rice, and soybean meal. Years of research go into these formulations to ensure Kitty gets just enough, but not too much, of each nutrient in the proper balance.

Reading the Label

Since commercial foods should provide the sole source of nutrition for your kitten, read the label information carefully to choose a good diet. Label information on pet foods must meet criteria established by the FDA, the U.S. Department of Agriculture, and the Federal Trade Commission. Most states also have stringent pet feed requirements, which are endorsed by the American Association of Feed Control Officials (AAFCO).

AAFCO is an advisory body composed of members from every state, and many states fashion pet food regulations after AAFCO's model feed bill. All pet foods involved in interstate commerce must, by law, disclose on their labels a guaranteed analysis, list of ingredients in descending order of weight, a statement about the food being adequate for a particular life stage, and validation of adequacy. These last two disclosures are what you should be looking for.

FEEDING LIFE STAGES

Kittens have different needs than do adult cats. Growing kittens require more protein, fat, calcium, phosphorus, magnesium, vitamin A and vitamin D than do mature felines. AAFCO has established nutritional guidelines for each life stage that cat foods must meet to be able to label the product "complete and balanced." Life stages are defined as *growth and reproduction* (for kittens and pregnant or nursing mothers), *maintenance* (adult cats), or *all life stages* (kittenhood, motherhood and adult).

Manufacturers must also validate, or prove, their claims. This can be done either by performing laboratory

---

READING THE CAT FOOD LABEL

Cats, like people, have certain specific nutritional requirements. For the most part, how well the different cat foods meet these needs has been ascertained through extensive testing by regulatory organizations, most notably the Association of American Feed Control Officials (AAFCO). When choosing a food for your cat, look for this type of statement on the label: "Animal feeding tests using AAFCO procedures." These foods were tested on cats.

When reviewing ingredients, remember they're listed in decreasing order by weight, which means the heavier, more abundant ingredients will be first. These include meats (or fish) and water. Remember, too, that cats are carnivores and must eat meat. They do not do well on a vegetarian diet. Ask your veterinarian or a cat breeder for dietary recommendations.

---

analysis or mathematical calculation, or by feeding trials. Just because chemical or computer analysis says ingredients should work doesn't mean your kitten's body will be able to use the food. Therefore, always choose a food that's been tested by AAFCO feeding trials. That means actual kittens have eaten and done well on the food.

The labels of kitten food products you choose should say, "Nutritionally complete and balanced for growth and reproduction (or all life stages) as substantiated through feeding trials in accordance with AAFCO procedures."

Professional breeders consider a cat a kitten until she's nine months old, but some cats continue growing after that. Your cat should remain on kitten formula as long as she's growing, for at least a year. Then, switch Kitty to adult rations. Kitten food contains more calories than adult food does, and a cat who has stopped growing can become overweight if she continues eating kitten food.

This is hard work, isn't it? Well, you can rest assured that all major manufacturers of cat food will meet your strict criteria. Now you only need to choose the brand.

The Best Brand

Generic/house brands are of inconsistent quality. These usually have the store name on the product. The word here is "cheap"—a product that is less expensive because it's composed of cheaper ingredients and is rarely tested in feeding trials. Even acceptable formulations often fall short on palatability because they are low in fat with little high-quality animal source protein. And if it doesn't tempt Kitty's appetite, she won't eat nearly enough. Since it's not as digestible, more waste ends up in the litter box rather than being used by your kitten.

Even though they seem economical, *avoid house-brand diets.* Provide quality nutrition from the beginning, and you'll have fewer expensive health problems that need veterinary attention down the road.

Name brands are also sold through grocery stores. They are usually formulated through feeding trials and are good products that can be trusted. Most cats and kittens do fine on name-brand foods, and some manufacturers also offer premium varieties.

Premium foods are often marketed through pet supply stores, dealers and animal hospitals. Premiums cost up to twice as much as other brands because they're made from costlier high-quality ingredients and go through the more expensive feeding trials.

Premium foods usually are extremely palatable due to a higher fat content. Higher digestibility and greater caloric density help reduce stool volume, a boon when it comes time to clean the litter box. The fact that the food is concentrated means your kitten doesn't need to eat as much, so the higher cost may be offset.

There are foods to feed all ages of your cat.

Choose either a name-brand or premium food for your new kitten. These products specialize in lines of quality food that provide a smooth transition when your kitten is old enough to graduate to adult rations.

Types of Food

Cat foods generally come in both dry and canned forms. Some kittens may have distinct preferences, while others may be easy to please.

Dry food is relatively inexpensive, storable without refrigeration, and very convenient to use. Dry cat food remains palatable and nutritious for up to twelve months, even after the bag has been opened. Dry foods are more likely to decrease the rate of tartar accumulation on kitty teeth.

Canned varieties are a little more expensive but extremely palatable, and they have high caloric density. They come in a variety of flavors to please the most finicky appetite. Canned food must be refrigerated after opening. It contains about seventy percent moisture, which partially fulfills your kitten's need for water. Unopened canned cat food will last nearly indefinitely, but most manufacturers recommend using canned products within two years.

Semimoist foods are packaged as individual servings and are convenient travel food, but they aren't appropriate for everyday use. They are kept moist by ingredients like corn syrup that bind water and prevent food from drying out. It's quite palatable, but the binding ingredient may cause your kitten to need to drink more water.

Scheduling Meals

Your kitten should be fed in the same place every day, and a bowl of clean, fresh water must be available at all times. Locate Kitty's food station some distance from the bathroom facilities, to avoid bruising sensitive feline sensibilities. Usually, a low-traffic end of the kitchen or laundry room works well. Each

---

GOOD AND BAD SNACKS

Besides feeding a high-quality commercial cat food, you can feed your cat some people foods— occasionally, and always as part of the cat's regular diet. Always consider total caloric intake and if you're going to treat Kitty, reduce his regular meal somewhat. Be careful what you give as treats. Here are some good ones (+) and bad ones (-):

+ vegetables, raw or cooked, without sauce

+ broth from water-packed meats and fish

+ cooked meat (poultry, beef, lamb, pork, liver), with any and all bones removed

+ cheese or yogurt

+ fresh fruit

- raw fish

- uncooked meats

- dog food

- bones of any kind

- chocolate in any form

- candies, desserts, sweets

- onions and raw potatoes

pet should have her own food bowl set some distance from the others.

The easiest feeding protocol is free-choice: You keep the bowl filled with more dry kibble than Kitty could possibly eat, and she nibbles at her convenience throughout the day.

DOG-PROOFING KITTY'S DOMAIN

Do you already have a dog? Even the best-trained pooch is tempted to sample cat food—or worse, clean up Kitty's aromatic bathroom deposits. To solve the problem, place Kitty's food and litter box where the dog can't reach them. For adult cats, elevating litter boxes and food bowls can be the answer, but tiny kittens less able to jump and climb need other options.

A covered litter box with an opening Kitty enters from below foils most dogs. Consider using two: one for Kitty's bathroom and the other to protect her food. Don't worry; Kitty will know which is which.

Try folding accordion-style baby gates to close off doorways or portions of rooms from Poochie. Choose one with lattice openings large enough for Kitty to go through, or cut a kitten-size opening too small for a dog.

Or, protect Kitty's domain with upside-down plastic milk crates placed over bowls and litter pans. Cutting a kitten-size opening lets her come and go but keeps snoopy Poochie out of her hair.

Free-Feeding

Most cats fed free-choice eat every few hours all day long, but they consume the same amount each day. Some adult cats don't know when to quit and continue to eat as long as the bowl is full. But obesity is not a problem in kittens, who need every mouthful of food they can get. Free-choice feeding works particularly well with growing kittens, who may not be able to eat enough in one serving to sustain them throughout a hard day's play.

Canned food spoils if left sitting in a bowl all day long, so it must be scheduled as meals. Measure the daily amount needed, divide it by three or four meals, and offer the food at the same times each day. Or, set out a bit more food than the entire daily amount, and allow Kitty to eat for up to thirty minutes; then pick up the bowl and put it back in the refrigerator until the next meal.

Probably the best method for kittens is a combination of free-choice and scheduled meals. Kittens younger than ten weeks old may have trouble with dry food. Feed canned food, or moisten kitten kibble with warm water (one ounce water to 1.5 cups food) until your baby is aggressively eating the diet. Set moistened dry food down three to four times a day, slowly reducing the amount of water until your kitten reaches ten weeks of age. Then you can leave dry food out all day.

Even if dry food is available at all times, you may wish to offer a spoonful or two of canned food in the morning and evening as a special treat. Be sure to pick it up after half an hour so that your kitten doesn't consume spoiled food and get a tummyache.

Cats prefer their food at room or body temperature, so a couple of seconds in the microwave will make refrigerated food more palatable. Eating cold food may cause your kitten to spit up, which may not bother her but will stain the carpet.

Canned food can't sit out all day, although a bowl of dry is good to munch on whenever.

Final Feeding Tips

Every form and flavor the ingenious human mind can devise tempts the palate of discriminating cat lovers. Yes, pet food marketing is aimed at people, not cats, for the very good reason that it's the two-legged customer who has the pocketbook.

For instance, advertisements focus on how tasty the diet looks or how your pet will relish a new flavor. *News flash:* Cats don't care how the food looks; as long as it smells good and the texture appeals to them, their food could be green octopus-shaped kibble and they'd chow down with gusto.

Neither does your kitten need or even crave variety in her diet. In the wild, a cat would be happy eating mice three times a day, 365 days a year. Despite information to the contrary, cats are creatures of habit who thrive on monotony. Commercial diets are composed of many ingredients that give Kitty more than enough variety. Choose a quality kitten food that Kitty likes to eat, and stick with it. Changing brands may create a finicky cat or, even worse, cause upset tummies.

It's dangerous, however, to try to starve a cat into eating something, so be cautious if you ever decide you need to change your kitten's diet. Kittens shouldn't go longer than eighteen to twenty-four hours without eating, while adult cats probably shouldn't exceed forty-eight hours without a meal. If your kitten is reluctant to eat a proffered food, mix in part of the old diet to ease her into the new ration.

Once weaned from mommy's milk, growing kittens need the nutrients in a kitten-formulated food.

A complete and balanced commercial diet provides all the nutrients your kitten needs. Remember, just because something's good for your kitten doesn't mean more is better. Vitamin supplements, commercial treats or table scraps can throw off the careful balance and cause nutritional difficulties. If you want to treat your kitten, use tidbits of nutritionally balanced canned food.

About Milk

Although milk is an excellent food source, it should never replace your kitten's water. Also, cow's milk and cat's milk contain different proteins. Some kittens past weaning don't have enough of the enzyme lactase to digest the milk sugar lactose, and the result is diarrhea.

That's no fun for you, your kitten or the carpet. It's best to avoid cow's milk and just stick to commercial kitten food.

The more you learn about feline nutrition, the better care you'll provide for your kitten. Don't leave the decision up to Kitty; after all, she'd probably prefer crunching crickets and munching mice.

Keeping Kitty Slim

As they age, cats—especially indoor cats—are prone to weight problems. This is because they exercise less and their metabolism slows down, just like us.

If you notice your cat's stomach area getting round and you have a hard time feeling the ribs through the flesh, your cat is or is getting fat. The first thing to do is consult with your veterinarian to first determine how bad the problem is, and second to discuss dietary changes. There are a number of "lite" cat foods on the market, and your veterinarian can assist you in choosing one. These foods contain more fiber and less fat, so they fill your cat up without filling him out.

Exercise is essential for all cats, and you don't need a feline fitness center to keep kitty in top shape. You will need to make a point of playing with your cat every day. There are tips for play and training in chapter 8, and suggestions for toys in chapter 4. A great toy for an all-around workout is the fish-pole toy, which you can use while you're sitting.

> **TUNAFISH**
>
> Cats find the strong fishy smell of tuna very appealing, tempting owners to feed it as a special treat or a preferred diet. But feeding a cat a lot of tuna can cause *steatitis*, a condition where vitamin E is destroyed by the excessive amounts of fatty acids in the food. Another potential problem is that the cat may decide it wants a tunafish-only diet, and will turn its nose up at regular cat food. Prevent these problems by feeding only very small amounts of tuna sporadically, as a treat. Make sure it is packed in water, not oil.

chapter 6

Grooming
Your
Kitten

No doubt you've seen your feline neatnik washing his whiskers. In fact, adult cats spend up to fifty percent of their awake time grooming themselves.

Hygiene is learned early, and kittens who aren't well cared for by Mom-cat frequently develop into unkempt adults. By the time kittens are two weeks old, they begin to lick themselves. Most kittens learn grooming techniques before they leave Mom, and they use their tongue, teeth and dampened forepaws and hind claws as kitty washrags and scratching/combing tools.

Despite your kitten's dedication to self-grooming, he'll need help cleaning hard-to-reach places. Longhair cats require more care than do shorthair kitties. Regular grooming helps reduce the amount of shed hair on your furniture or that's swallowed by the cat to become hairballs spit up on the carpet.

Dry indoor heat stimulates house cats to shed pretty much all the time, and only the removal of loose hair will keep longhair kitty coats unmatted. A matted coat is not only painful for the cat when it pulls tender skin, but it also provides a perfect flea environment.

Grooming is a wonderful opportunity to examine your kitten for unusual lumps and bumps; ear, eye or claw problems; and parasites or skin problems. It also helps strengthen the bond between you and your pet.

Your kitten will look forward to regular overall grooming sessions.

To your kitten, grooming just plain feels good and is a way of expressing affection.

Cleaning Your Kitten

Once- or twice-weekly grooming will keep most kitty coats in fine form. Regular brushing and combing takes only five minutes or so. *But be warned:* Kitty may get addicted to the wonderful attention, in which case you won't be able to groom too much.

Cats thrive on routine, so set aside a special time and place for grooming, and stick to the schedule. To begin, spread a white sheet or towel on a table, or on the floor between your knees, and set Kitty on top. Use a white sheet so it's easier to tell if debris that has fallen from your cat's coat is just dirt or is something problematic.

Start with Petting

Always start with petting. Get Kitty's motor rumbling by running your fingers through his fur. Not only will he enjoy the attention, you'll find mats or burrs ahead of time and avoid a painful ripping encounter with the comb or brush. Finger-combing also familiarizes you with the angles and planes of your cat's body. Running a comb rudely across a bony spine or into tender nipples will aggravate Kitty, who will abruptly cut the session short.

Establish a Pattern

Some groomers begin with the tail and flanks, then work their way forward to the sides, tummy, neck and face. Others reverse the procedure. Establish your own routine, as long as you cover the whole cat. Start and end each session grooming the part of your kitten he particularly enjoys, like his throat or cheeks.

Get your kitten used to the equipment by letting him sniff and investigate or even play with the comb or brush. For shorthair kittens, use the soft-bristle or rubber curry brush, then finish with the flea comb. Always work in the direction in which the fur grows.

For longhair kittens, use the widest teeth on your greyhound comb. Kitty appreciates an initially light touch and short strokes, and he will arch his back into the comb to let you know how good grooming feels. On subsequent strokes, comb through clear to the skin. Then switch to the narrower-toothed comb and repeat the process. Finish your longhair beauty with the slicker brush.

Check for any buggy intruders your kitten may pick up.

Let Kitty Be Your Guide

Think of scratching the skin rather than combing the fur, and make grooming an extension of petting. Let the kitten be your guide. It's better if your kitten asks for more rather than complaining you've gone too far.

66

Hold grooming sessions to only a minute or two, and stop before your cat demands it; then finish at a later time. By continuing to groom a reluctant cat, you reinforce his discomfort and turn the whole experience into one he dreads rather than one he looks forward to. You want grooming to be fun. Finish each session with a favorite game.

Grooming gloves available at most pet supply stores are a pleasant shortcut, but they don't take the place of through-to-the-skin sessions. Tiny nibs in the palm collect shed fur as you pet your kitten. Another alternative is an old nylon stocking. Slip half a nylon stocking over your hand, and simply pet the cat to leave his coat shiny and remove lots of shed hair.

Messy Mats

Longhairs typically mat behind the ears, under the chin, and in the armpits of all four legs. Some also get nasty mats in their "britches" beneath the tail where feces or litter may catch.

Never use scissors to cut out a mat, or you run the risk of cutting the thin, tender skin as your kitten squirms. Instead, use a wide-toothed comb and start from the hair tips at the end of the mat; then work progressively deeper and deeper. Rub a bit of cornstarch into the mat to help untangle the fur, then comb again. Try threading the wide-tooth comb through the mat to prevent painful pulling; then brush over it with your slicker brush. If all else fails, use an electric razor to break up the mat. You may need a professional groomer's help.

HAIRBALLS

To cats, grooming is a way of life. They are clean creatures who use their specially designed tongues to both keep their hair and skin debris-free and to cover themselves with scent. Hairballs are accumulations of the loose fur the cat swallows as it grooms. This fur either travels through the cat's digestive system and is defecated, or it irritates the system and is vomited out.

You can help keep hairballs to a minimum by combing out your cat's loose hair. If she becomes constipated anyway, you can put a small amount of petroleum jelly on her paws to lick off (cats like the taste). But with regular combing from you and regular grooming by them, cats can handle their hairballs naturally. Anything unusual should be reported to your veterinarian.

Regular grooming should prevent embarrassing and painful mats from developing. *Be warned:* A thorough combing and the removal of mats is a must before bathing; otherwise, the water will make the mats as hard as cement, and to remove them you will have to shave them off.

If Your Kitten Has Fleas

After combing or brushing your kitten, examine the white cloth grooming surface. So-called "flea dirt" looks like black dots and will be caught by the towel, alerting you that parasites have moved in. Uh oh, that means Kitty needs a flea treatment.

Regular grooming and attention are the best flea preventatives.

Particular care must be taken with kittens when treating them for fleas, because the insecticides that poison the bugs can also kill your kitten. Cats are more susceptible to insecticides than dogs are, and kittens are the most sensitive of all. Safe products are available from pet stores and from your veterinarian, but you must read the label and follow all the directions. Only use products that actually say *safe for kittens.* Even some of the so-called "natural" citrus-based products with d-limonene can be toxic to your kitten.

COMB THEM OUT

For controlling fleas on your kitten, a flea comb is the safest way to go. The narrow teeth catch and comb the bugs out. Prepare a bowl of soapy water, and comb your kitten with short strokes. Dip the comb in the water to drown the caught fleas.

The next-safest route is to use products containing pyrethrin, which is probably the least toxic insecticide available for use on kittens. Use a shampoo for an initial flea kill, and in between baths use a kitten-safe spray. Spray the product on a cotton ball, and first wipe it carefully around the face and neck, then over the body.

You must also treat your kitten's environment to keep new buggy hitchhikers from catching a ride. For more flea-control tips, refer to the section on flea treatment in chapter 7.

Bathing Your Kitten

Yes, bathing a cat is not only necessary at times; it can be done without permanently traumatizing you or your kitten. Some cats actually like the water, while most can learn to tolerate bathing with a minimum of fuss.

Kittens should not be bathed until they are at least four weeks old. Younger kittens have trouble regulating their temperature and can easily be chilled and develop pneumonia. For touch-ups and spot cleaning between baths, commercial waterless cat shampoos are available that don't require rinsing. Pour the product on a soft cloth and rub it into the coat, then comb it out. The kitten is never submerged but feels like he's being stroked.

Sometimes, nothing will suffice but an all-out dunking. There are three basic cat-bathing methods: the shower, the pan, and the bucket. No matter which technique you choose, get everything ready ahead of time before introducing Kitty to the idea.

PREPPING THE PLACE

The room should be warm and draft-free. Bathrooms are ideal, but a double kitchen sink works well for small kittens, too. Get all the breakables and scary stuff like shower curtains put away or looped out of reach. Remember to remove your jewelry and to wear old clothes. You'll need a washcloth for Kitty's face, two or more dry towels and kitten shampoo at the ready.

Run the water before you bring in the victim . . . er, your kitten. The water should be kitten-temperature, about 102 degrees.

Your kitten will feel great when he's all clean.

The Shower Method Place a towel or rubber mat in the bottom of the sink for a foothold. (If you are bathing a larger kitten in a tub, stand him on plastic milk crates so that he will have something to grab and you will be able to reach underneath him to rinse his tummy.) While keeping one hand on your kitten, use a hand-held spray attachment to wet the fur thoroughly, avoiding the face. Holding the nozzle against the body is less upsetting to your kitten.

Never spray your kitten in the face; you wouldn't like it, and neither will he. Use a washcloth to wet and wash the face, and avoid getting soap in his eyes, mouth, nose or ears. You want to make the experience as positive and unstressful as possible.

Talk to your kitten soothingly, or perhaps play soft music to help calm him. Flea shampoos should be applied around the kitten's neck first, to make a sudsy barrier that prevents fleas from hiding in the ears and facial fur. Lather Kitty's body, legs, feet and tail. If the shampoo is for fleas, the lather must set for up to ten minutes.

Stay with your kitten to make sure a sudsy projectile doesn't escape the sink and get soapsuds on the floor.

Try wrapping your bubbly kitty in a towel, and hold him for the prescribed time. Then rinse him, using the washrag to eliminate shampoo from his face. Feed water gently onto his fur, starting at the neck and letting it sluice suds off the fur. Once you're sure all the soap is gone, rinse him one more time; any shampoo left will dry out the coat and skin and cause dandruff.

The Bucket/Pan Methods   For kittens who are upset by spraying water, the bucket or pan method may be less stressful. For bigger kittens, use buckets or wastebaskets set in the bathtub. Smaller dishwashing pans or even the double kitchen sink works well for little ones. If you're working in the kitchen, you'll need a towel or drip-pan handy on the counter, too.

Fill two or three containers with kitten-temperature water. The water level should reach your kitten's neck as he stands on his hind legs and clutches the side of the container.

Grasp your kitten beneath the chest with one hand, while supporting his furry bottom in the other, and slowly lower him in the first basin of water. Avoid splashing, since that's what upsets cats the most. Usually, the kitten will grab the edge of the container as he stands on his hind legs, but he won't get too irritated unless his face gets wet. The edge of the container gives him something to do with his paws, other than clawing your arm.

Continue supporting the kitten's chest as you work the water into his coat with your other hand. Lift out the kitten and set him in the tub (or on the towel or drip-pan on the counter); then add shampoo and suds him up. Use a washcloth on his face.

Dip the scrubbed, sudsy kitten back into the first container, still supporting his chest, and rinse him thoroughly. Lift him out, and use your free hand to squeegee water off his fur. Then, repeat the dip and squeegee process in the second bucket or sink, and again in the third. Rinse his face with the washcloth.

FINISHING TOUCHES

For cats who detest both the shower and the dunking, simply fill shallow containers with a few inches of water. The process is similar to that involved in the bucket method, but you use a sponge or cup to wet the fur.

Finally, wrap your kitten in a warm, dry towel and blot up as much water as possible. Kittens catch cold easily and must be kept warm until completely dry. Shorthair kitties dry quickly, but longer fur can take several hours and may need the help of a blow dryer. Use only the lowest setting, or it can get too hot and burn tender kitten skin. To give your longhair that striking full-coated look, comb and lift the fur as you blow-dry.

Paws That Claw: Nail Care

When your kitten walks, her claws rarely touch the ground, and she does not wear them down naturally even by using the scratching post. Overgrown claws can split, break off and bleed, or they can tear when caught by carpeting or furniture. Claw maintenance prevents problems from happening.

The best time to start claw maintenance is before your kitten actually needs it. With tiny kittens, simply go through the motions to get Kitty used to having her paws handled. On young kittens, human nail clippers work fine, and there are also those available at pet stores or veterinary offices.

ROUTINE GROOMING

These are the things you should do at least once a week to keep your kitten looking and feeling her best:

brush kitty

comb kitty

check skin, eyes, ears and paws for problem spots

clip nails

check teeth and gums

play with kitty afterward!

Cat claws are like human fingernails and are made of dead protein that has no feeling. The nerves are in the quick, inside the claw at the root, which shows through pink. The portion you clip is white or clear. Never cut into the pink portion, which is very tender and can bleed. Clip off only the curved white or clear tip, and you'll be safe.

This process works best if two people participate. Have somebody hold your kitten on a table or in his or her lap. You can then grasp each leg firmly in turn, gently squeeze the paw pad to express the claws, and clip the nails with the other hand. Check carefully to be sure you didn't nick the quick. If there is any bleeding, scrape the claw through a bar of soap. Use an emery board to smooth any rough edges.

Reward your kitten for being so good by having a fun play session. Plan to trim the nails at least once a month, preferably the day before bathing. Each time the nails are trimmed, the quick recedes a bit, making it less likely that you'll quick the cat.

Dental Hygiene

Just like human teeth, cat teeth that aren't properly cared for get dirty, cause gum disease and bad breath, and can ultimately decay and abscess, causing much pain. Although many cats and their owners resist the notion of dental care, you *should* think about providing your kitten with regular dental maintenance to help prevent serious problems and keep her mouth healthy. Start regular teeth cleaning now, once or twice weekly, to get her used to the notion.

At about five months of age, she will have most of her permanent teeth. *Do not brush them with people toothpaste;* it can upset her stomach. Use plain water or a special commercial cat toothpaste.

Massage her teeth and gums in a circular motion, using a very soft baby toothbrush or a piece of gauze wrapped about your finger. Cleaning the outside of the teeth is most helpful, since she uses her tongue to clean the inside. Keep sessions short, perhaps only doing one side of the mouth at a sitting. Always reward your kitten by playing with her.

Eye Care

Kittens with flatter faces, like Persian-type breeds, have prominent eyes that tend to tear. This can lead to a cosmetic problem if tears stain the fur beneath the eyes of light-faced kittens.

The problem can also be more serious: If not gently cleaned away, the normal secretions can dry on the fur and cause the eyes and lids to become inflamed or even infected. Tears should be clear and liquid, not thick or dark-colored, both of which indicate illness.

Gently wipe out the corners of the kitten's eyes with cotton balls soaked with saline. Daily attention will help prevent staining. Pet stores also have kitten-safe products for removing the stain.

Ear Care

Examine your kitten's ears every week. The inside should be pink and relatively clean; a small amount of honey-colored wax is normal. If the wax is very thick or dark and crumbly, your kitten may have parasites, which must be treated by your veterinarian.

For normal maintenance, use an ear-cleaning solution available from your veterinarian or pet store, or a bit of baby oil. Don't put anything inside the ear; simply swab the visible portion with a cotton ball soaked with the solution. You can also carefully use cotton swabs to clean all the little crevices, but be cautious; you risk damaging the ears if you probe too far down.

chapter 7

Keeping
Your
Kitten
Healthy

Your kitten's health depends on the working partnership between you and your veterinarian. To start off on the right paw, your kitten should be evaluated by a veterinarian as soon as you get her.

People become veterinarians because they care about and want to serve animals, but some practices or individuals may suit your needs better than others. Whatever facility you choose, you

must feel comfortable with your veterinarian, who should always be willing to answer your questions. Only then will it be a true partnership that best benefits your kitten.

Advances in feline health and medicine are being made constantly. This chapter is only a guide, and is meant to help you diagnose and understand your kitten's ailments; always consult your veterinarian for the most current information.

Preventive Health Care

Prevention is truly the best cure and should be used to ensure a happy, healthy life for your new kitten. The idea is simple: prevent illnesses from developing or spreading by following basic health-care principles. These include vaccinating your kitten against infectious diseases; keeping routine appointments with your veterinarian so he or she can monitor the overall health of your kitten; and keeping close tabs on your kitten yourself, checking skin, teeth, fur, eyes, ears and mood. These simple preventive procedures will save you in dollars, time and heartache.

Kittens should be vaccinated to protect them against certain diseases.

VACCINATIONS

Kittens are particularly susceptible to disease because their immune systems are immature. They are protected from infection when maternal antibodies received from Mom's first milk (colostrum) are present in high-enough amounts.

But these same maternal antibodies also neutralize preventive vaccinations, which is why kittens are given a series of vaccinations instead of just one. Colostrum protection gradually declines over the first twelve weeks as the kitten's own immune system matures and takes over. When Mom's protection begins to wane and Kitty's hasn't yet fully matured, kittens are at the highest risk from infectious disease—and most susceptible to the benefits of vaccination.

To be fully protected, your kitten needs a series of vaccinations two to three weeks apart, starting when she's six to eight weeks old and continuing until she's fourteen to sixteen weeks of age. Once the series has been completed, yearly vaccinations protect adult cats thereafter. Currently, four vaccinations are available to protect your kitten from preventable illnesses.

A trustworthy veterinarian with whom you can discuss things is key to your cat's good health.

A combination shot protects the kitten against feline distemper and upper respiratory virus diseases. A 3-in-1 vaccination combines protection against feline distemper, feline calicivirus, and feline herpesvirus. And a **4-in-1** also includes feline chlamydiosis.

The **FeLV vaccination** protects cats against feline leukemia virus infection. Initially, a small sample of your kitten's blood is tested to be sure she's healthy, since FeLV won't protect her if she's already infected with the disease. When the result is negative, the kitten receives two vaccinations about three weeks apart, then is revaccinated yearly thereafter.

The **FIP vaccination** against feline infectious peritonitis initially requires two doses three to four weeks apart, and then yearly thereafter. Unlike the others, the FIP vaccine is not an injection but is administered as nose drops.

A **rabies vaccination** is recommended for all cats and required by law in many states. Kittens typically are first given a rabies shot at age sixteen weeks, then are revaccinated either annually or every three years, depending on the local laws.

Common Diseases

UPPER RESPIRATORY INFECTION

Cats are susceptible to upper respiratory infections because they inhale viruses and bacteria as they sniff interesting smells. These diseases are caused by *Feline Viral Rhinotracheitis (FVR)*; *Feline Calicivirus (FCV)*; and the bacterial infection *Chlamydia*, also called pneumonitis.

Vaccinating your kitten will protect her from various diseases.

The most common sign is sneezing, but coughing, runny eyes and nose and even painful eye and mouth ulcers can develop. Severe disease can lead to pneumonia. There is no cure; treatment is limited to symptomatic and supportive care. Recovered cats become carriers for life and can transmit disease to other healthy cats during "flare-ups" brought on by stress.

Disease is primarily spread by direct cat-to-cat contact, aerosol (sneezing), and by contact with contaminated items like cages, food bowls and litter boxes. The virus can also be carried on human skin, which means you may spread the infection by simply petting your cats.

FELINE DISTEMPER

This type of feline parvovirus, also called *Feline Panleukopenia*, isn't related to canine distemper at all. Signs include depression, fever, loss of appetite, diarrhea and vomiting and dehydration. Ninety to 100 percent of unvaccinated cats exposed to the virus will die.

Recovered cats may become carriers able to infect other unprotected cats. The virus is extremely contagious and is transmitted orally through contact with infected surfaces like food bowls or litter boxes. The virus can live in the environment for months to years and is resistant to most common disinfectants.

FELINE LEUKEMIA VIRUS (FELV)

The leading infectious cause of death in cats in the United States, this virus compromises the cat's immune system, making FeLV-infected cats more susceptible to other diseases. Most cats die within three years of infection from related diseases like leukemia (cancer of the blood cells), cancer of the lymph system or anemia.

Any major medical problem can indicate FeLV infection. But infected cats may show no symptoms for years, yet can be shedding the virus and infecting other cats. The disease is spread by cat-to-cat contact, through shared dishes and litter boxes, or even from an infected mother cat to her unborn kittens.

The virus is extremely fragile and does not survive long in the environment. It can be destroyed by common household products like detergents, alcohol and bleach. Preventing contact with strange cats eliminates exposure.

FELINE INFECTIOUS PERITONITIS (FIP)

Caused by a feline corona virus, this is the second leading infectious cause of death in cats. FIP has no known cure, and there is still much to be learned about this deadly disease. Once a cat is infected, she will die.

Cats become infected by inhaling or swallowing the virus, thought to be shed in the saliva, urine and feces of infected cats. Cats allowed outdoors, those raised in multiple cat households, and cats who are stressed from infection, malnutrition or overcrowding are at the highest risk for the disease. Very old and very young cats also seem affected more often.

The effusive, or "wet," form of the disease results in a progressive, painless swelling of the abdomen with fluid. Fluid may also accumulate in the chest cavity and make breathing difficult. The noneffusive, or "dry," form of the disease causes incoordination and partial or complete paralysis of hind legs, convulsions, personality changes and eye disease. Some cats may have a combination of the wet and dry forms of FIP.

FELINE IMMUNODEFICIENCY VIRUS (FIV)

Make sure your kitten gets regular veterinary check-ups.

This lentevirus belongs to the same family as the human immunodeficiency virus (HIV) that causes AIDS. The viruses are species specific, which means people cannot get the cat virus, nor can cats be infected by the human disease.

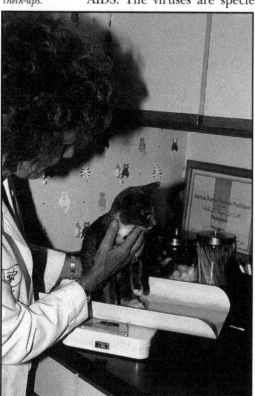

The disease is most commonly transmitted through bites. Male cats and free-roaming outdoor cats are at highest risk, although kittens can be exposed by their infected mother when she bites through the umbilical cord directly after their birth.

Cats with the disease first show only vague signs like anemia or recurrent fever. As FIV progresses, cats begin to lose weight; develop enlarged lymph nodes; and often suffer secondary illnesses, including upper respiratory infections, bladder and kidney infections and severe gum infections.

There is no treatment for this fatal disease, and currently no protective vaccinations are available. The only way to protect your kitten is to prevent exposure to other cats who might be infected.

RABIES

Caused by a virus that attacks the brain, rabies affects virtually all mammals, including humans, but today the cat is the most commonly infected pet in the United States.

Rabies is transmitted by direct animal-to-animal contact, usually through a bite. It generally takes three to eight weeks for symptoms to appear, which are similar to those caused by meningitis. Animals first stop eating and drinking, and seek solitude. Then they either show signs of paralysis or become vicious. Once symptoms develop, rabies is always fatal, and victims should be euthanized to avoid their suffering an agonizing death or infecting anyone else.

LOWER URINARY TRACT DISEASE (LUTD)

This is actually a group of disorders with various causes that can result in serious urologic difficulties in cats. Adult cats are at the highest risk, but older kittens may be affected.

The most serious condition is blockage by crystals and/or mucus that prevents the cat from voiding urine. LUTD has been linked to diet and more recently to stress. Today virtually all commercial cat foods are formulated to reduce the risk of LUTD.

FELINE UROLOGIC SYNDROME (FUS)

FUS is the name given to a range of disorders of the lower urinary tract in cats. These disorders are of *unknown origin*, but cause urethral obstruction or painful, difficult or bloody urination. Cats with FUS tend to urinate often and may vocalize while urinating (a sign of pain). If you notice any of these signs, get your cat to the veterinarian as soon as possible.

Many cat foods claim to lessen the risk of FUS by using less ash in their foods. Ash is what remains when a sample of the food is burned for chemical and nutritional analysis. Ash contains many minerals, and researchers suspect magnesium may be a culprit where FUS is concerned. Therefore, some manufacturers are reducing the amount of ash in their foods, usually by reducing the bone meal content. Besides consulting with your veterinarian about the best food for your kitten, remember to provide plenty of water, and to not let your kitty get fat, which strains the kidneys.

Warning signs include bloody urine, urine with a strong ammonia odor, squatting or straining and crying at the end of urination, and listlessness, poor appetite, and/ or excessive thirst. Any blockage must be seen immediately by a veterinarian. Coma and death will occur within seventy-two hours of complete obstruction.

Home Health Exam

An important part of preventive care is to check your kitten regularly for signs of problems. These could include strange bumps, cuts, scabs, runny nose, discharge in the eyes, sneezing, drooling, swelling, hair loss, lethargy, irritability, incontinence— anything out of the ordinary.

The vet will thoroughly examine your kitten, including looking inside the ears.

TEMPERATURE

A healthy cat or kitten's body temperature is between 100.4 and 102.5 degrees Fahrenheit. Take your kitten's temperature a few different times while it's perfectly healthy so you can learn what your kitten's normal temperature is.

To take a cat's temperature, ask an adult friend or family member for help. One of you should take the temperature while the other one holds the kitten, talks to her and reassures her. For the person taking the temperature, use a human rectal thermometer. Put a small amount of petroleum jelly on the tip to lubricate it. Gently hold your kitten's tail up and insert the thermometer about one inch into the rectum. Leave the thermometer in for two minutes, then slide it out, wipe with a tissue, and read. Report anything unusual to your veterinarian.

PULSE

A cat's pulse runs between 160 and 240 beats per minute. As with temperature, you should learn the pulse rate for your particular cat while she's at rest and in good health so you'll know what's normal. To do this, feel along the cat's chest just behind the foreleg. The skin is thin there and you should be able to feel the pulse. Put two fingertips on it and count the beats while you watch the second hand on your watch tick away one minute.

BODY WORK

While you're petting or grooming your cat, move your fingertips all the way down to the skin and feel all over the body. You're feeling for lumps, scratches, rough spots, dry areas, inflammation or localized pain. Include legs, feet and tail.

Pay particular attention to the head. Look at your cat's eyes. Are they shiny and clear? How about the ears. Are they pink and healthy looking with no waxy debris or dirt? Is your cat's nose running? Try to push back the lips and examine the teeth. Are they white and whole or do you see tartar build-up or possibly a chipped tooth? Again, anything unusual should be passed along to your veterinarian for consultation.

Examine your cat's claws. Do they need trimming? (See chapter 6 for instructions on clipping nails.)

Don't forget to look at your cat's urogenital area. Do you notice any peculiar discharge, swelling, crusting or redness?

Last but not least, learn your cat's body language, preferences and habits. Cats are good at hiding signs of illness, and knowing what's normal for your cat will help you notice when something's off. Here are some things to look for:

- Dull coat or scraggly appearance

- Excessive drinking

- Loss of appetite for up to three days

- Diarrhea for more than one day

- Trouble eliminating or inappropriate elimination

- Blood in the urine or feces

- Coughing, wheezing or excessive sneezing

- Sudden weight change (increase or decrease)

- Unusual discharge from eyes or nose

- Hair loss

- Sudden behavior change—unusually aggressive or passive

Anything unusual or worrisome warrants a call to your veterinarian. For emergencies like bleeding or shock, see the section on emergencies and first aid later in this chapter.

Intestinal Parasites

Intestinal parasites, those disgusting worms, are often more distressing to you than to your kitten. Outdoor cats run the highest risk of contracting them, but any cat showing one or more of the following signs should be examined for parasites. Learning about these nasty freeloaders should give you the necessary ammunition to protect your kitten.

ROUNDWORMS

Nearly all kittens will have roundworms acquired from their mothers' milk, from contaminated soil, or from eating infected animals or insects. Severely infected kittens may have a potbellied appearance, a dull coat, diarrhea, or mucus in the stool, and they may cough and lose their appetite. You may find spaghetti-like worms coiled in Kitty's stool or vomit.

Veterinary diagnosis is made by identifying eggs during microscopic examination of a stool sample. Many veterinarians recommend worming all kittens for roundworms, and two doses of a liquid oral medication usually are given two weeks apart.

HOOKWORMS

These are a more serious parasite that can cause severe anemia. Signs include weight loss, diarrhea, vomiting, listlessness and lack of energy. In young kittens, hookworms can cause sudden collapse and death.

Cats are infected by ingesting eggs found in feces, and hookworm larvae are also able to penetrate the skin to infect a cat. Adult worms are tiny, less than one-half-inch long, and can't be seen in the feces. Diagnosis is made by identifying eggs during microscopic examination of the stool. The same treatment for roundworms also eliminates hookworms.

TAPEWORM

These are the most common intestinal parasites seen in cats. Tapeworms require an intermediate host, the flea, for transmission. Cats become infected by grooming away and swallowing fleas.

Composed of a chain of small segments built from the neck down, tapeworms can grow to more than a foot in length. Each segment contains several hundred eggs, and when mature, the segments break away and are passed in the stool.

Diagnosis is made when segments are found wiggling in the litter box, the anal area of the pet's fur or perhaps your kitten's favorite spot on the sofa. Dried segments look like grains of rice.

Diarrhea and occasionally blood are seen with tapeworms, and very large numbers can cause partial blockage. Pills or shots are available to eliminate infections, but the best prevention is flea control. Some veterinarians recommend tapeworm treatment for any cat with fleas.

COCCIDIA

This protozoal parasite colonizes and attacks the lining of the intestine. Kittens and cats can be infected by coming into contact with an infected animal's stool or by eating infected rodents.

The signs may come and go, and include bloody and loose stool with a lot of mucus. Diagnosis is made by microscopic examination of a stool sample. Your veterinarian will prescribe either a liquid or pill medication to eliminate the problem.

GIARDIA

This is another protozoa that infects the small intestine. Cats transmit giardia to each other through contact with feces, food or water. The parasite causes chronic diarrhea, and affected cats may also have a poor hair coat and a distended stomach from gas. Diagnosis is sometimes difficult, and giardia is best diagnosed and treated by your veterinarian.

Other Parasites
EAR MITES

These are the most common cause of ear disease in cats and kittens. These tiny parasites may infest your kitten's ear and cause extreme irritation that can lead to infection. They crawl through the ear canal and bite the skin to feed on lymph.

Affected kittens scratch their ears and shake their heads, and often have a dark crumbly or tarry substance inside the ear. Left untreated, ear mites can progress to inflammation and infection. Your veterinarian will diagnose the problem and prescribe the appropriate treatment.

HEARTWORMS

These blood parasites are transmitted by mosquitos. They primarily affect dogs but can also infect cats. Mosquitos pick up baby worms, called microfilaria, by biting an infected dog. When the infected mosquito bites another pet, heartworm larvae enter the skin. They migrate to the victim's heart or pulmonary artery, where they mature and complete their life cycle by shedding microfilaria into the bloodstream. Heartworms interfere with blood circulation and heart function. Infected cats often show no signs, then suddenly collapse and die. Others vomit intermittently.

Outdoor middle-aged cats are at highest risk, but exposure can take place during kittenhood. Unlike dogs, cats tend not to have baby worms in the blood, which makes diagnosis very difficult. To become infected, cats must live in an area where infected dogs provide microfilariae, and where mosquitos have a taste for both cats and dogs. If heartworms are a problem for dogs in your area, medications are available from your veterinarian that will prevent your kitten from becoming infected.

FLEAS

The top complaint of pet owners, fleas are more than mere itchy aggravations. They can transmit disease and cause severe allergic reactions.

Blood loss from fleas can kill your kitten. Signs include lethargy, reluctance to play and loss of appetite. See your veterinarian immediately if the normally pink areas around your kitten's eyes and ears are very pale.

FIGHTING FLEAS

Remember that the fleas you see on your kitten are only part of the problem—the smallest part of the problem. To rid your kitten and home of fleas, you need to treat the animal and your home. Here's how:

Identify where your kitten(s) sleeps. These are "hot spots."

Clean your kitten's bedding regularly by vacuuming and washing.

Spray "hot spots" with a nontoxic, long-lasting flea larvicide.

If your kitten spends time outdoors, treat her favorite haunts ("hot spots") with insecticide.

Kill flea eggs on kittens with a product containing insect growth regulators (IGRs).

Kill fleas on your kitten per your veterinarian's recommendation.

There are no easy answers to flea control, but to beat the bugs you must first understand flea biology. Adult fleas mate on Kitty and remain there unless involuntarily dislodged. A blood meal stimulates egg laying; ten female fleas can produce 250,000 offspring in thirty days.

Most eggs fall from Kitty into the environment. In one to fourteen days, eggs hatch into tiny maggotlike larvae. In another three weeks, larvae spin cocoons, then later emerge as adults. The complete life cycle takes thirty days or less, and fleas may live from a few weeks to more than a year. They can survive months without feeding, and can even remain frozen for a year and revive.

RESTRAINING YOUR KITTEN

Cats are escape artists, and if they don't want to be held, they will squirm right out of your hands. If you need to examine your kitten closely and she's not cooperating, try these techniques.

1. *For a somewhat cooperative kitten:* Place one hand under your kitten's lower jaw with thumb on one side, fingers on the other. Don't hold too tightly! Use your other hand to check your kitten. If there's someone to help you, you can use your other hand to hold one of kitty's front paws while the other person examines her.

2. *If your kitten is uncooperative:* If you're by yourself, grasp your kitten's fur behind the neck. This is what Mom did to immobilize kitty if she had to be moved. If you have a helper, grasp the fur behind the neck and pick up a front paw.

Medicating Your Cat

Cats don't always take kindly to taking their medicine, and it's almost impossible to fool a cat into swallowing a pill surrounded by even the tastiest of treats.

When your veterinarian prescribes medication for your cat, ask him or her which would be the easiest form to administer, pill or liquid. Some drugs come in both forms, some in one or the other.

GIVING PILLS

The first thing you'll want to do is get a plush towel to wrap around your cat while you hold him in your lap and give him the pill. That way his legs will be immobilized. With the cat firmly in the towel on your lap, grasp his head above the jaws and tilt the head back. Press against the sides of the mouth with your forefinger and thumb so he opens his mouth. With head back and mouth open, place or drop the pill as far back in the throat as you can. Release instantly, then put your hand over his head so he won't try to spit the pill out. Stroke the throat until you see him swallow. Then give him a special treat and let him go.

If this is impossible, ask your veterinarian for a pill-gun, a hard plastic contraption that substitutes for your fingers and "shoots" the pill to the back of the throat.

GIVING LIQUIDS

Liquids come with droppers you fill up with medicine then squirt into the back of the mouth. You will probably need to use the towel with this method as well, since cats don't especially like the taste of the medicine and will struggle.

APPLYING OINTMENT

Your veterinarian may prescribe an ointment for a wound or skin condition. If the ointment is applied somewhere the cat can lick it, chances are it won't do the job. Your veterinarian may suggest you put an Elizabethan collar on your cat. This is a horn-shaped piece of plastic that attaches to your cat's collar and keeps him from being able to lick himself.

Skin Problems

ALLERGIES

Allergies are the immune system's response to an irritant. The immune system protects the cat from invasions of bacteria, viruses and other infectious organisms. Survival would be impossible without it. But the immune system is also triggered by irritants as varied as pollen, hair spray, certain fabrics, dust or insect bites. These irritants cause swelling, sneezing, itching, closing of the eyelids, diarrhea or vomitting.

The irritating substances are called allergens, and they enter the system through the lungs, digestive tract, injection (a bug bite, for example) or simple skin exposure. As long as the cat continues to be exposed to the allergen, it will continue to have an allergic reaction. It is sometimes difficult to determine exactly what the allergen is. Cats with allergies suffer, and must be taken to the veterinarian, where tests can be performed to determine the source of the allergen and a sufficient treatment.

RINGWORM

Though several "worms" have already been discussed in this chapter, this one is not a parasite. Rather, it is a fungal infection that leaves a circle (ring) of hair loss and scaly skin. There is sometimes a red ring at the margin of the spot. Ringworm itself doesn't itch, but when the dry, scaly skin breaks into sores, it can cause itching. Ringworm is contagious between species, so any pet in the household can transmit it to another pet or to a person. If you notice a bald spot on your cat, you should have it checked for ringworm. Your veterinarian will prescribe treatment.

FELINE ACNE

Some cats develop pimple-like bumps or blackheads under their chins. This is feline acne and is more common in cats with oily skin. There are special shampoos and ointments to treat this condition.

LUMPS AND BUMPS

Another name for a lump or bump is a tumor. There are two types of tumors: malignant and benign. Malignant tumors are cancerous; benign tumors are not. The only way to tell the difference is to have the lump tested. The sooner a malignant tumor is diagnosed, the greater the chance for removal and complete recovery. That's why it's important to note any suspicious bumps and report them to your veterinarian immediately.

Of course, there are lumps and bumps caused by such diverse things as bruises, cuts or insect bites. These lumps are usually painful to the touch and you may be able to see the stinger or scratch on it. Depending on their severity, these can be treated with antibiotic ointment and regular cleansing.

Declawing Your Cat

Cat owners may resort to declawing surgery when unable to dissuade Kitty from clawing the furniture. This surgery is painful for the cat, irreversible and more of a convenience for you than a benefit to the cat. Cats without claws aren't able to climb or protect themselves as well and should never be allowed outdoors.

Before considering declawing, first try the training and behavior-modification techniques described in chapters 9 and 10. Another alternative is claw covers, which are polyvinyl tips that are glued to each claw to prevent damage to furniture. They are available from veterinarians, shelters and pet supply stores, and last six weeks before being shed as the claw grows. Nail covers are applied by technicians, or you can learn to apply them yourself.

If it comes down to getting rid of the claws or getting rid of the kitten (horrors!), then certainly declawing procedures should be considered. Veterinarians prefer to perform the operation on young cats, twelve to sixteen weeks old.

Usually, the surgery is performed only on the front paws and consists of the surgical amputation of the last bone of each toe that includes the claw. A newer, supposedly less-stressful procedure is called a tendonectomy, in which the tendon of each front toe is clipped so that the claw cannot be extended.

Most cats sail through the surgery with flying colors. But there can be complications or infections, and a few cats resort to biting when they no longer have claws with which to protect themselves.

Spaying or Neutering

Your kitten should be spayed or neutered. PERIOD.

Spaying or neutering (altering) refers to the surgical removal of an animal's reproductive organs. Despite Kitty's biological urges to the contrary, there are already too many kittens being born.

It's estimated that four kittens out of each litter of five will not find a good home. That warm, fuzzy wonder you're cuddling is the lucky fifth. Preventing the births of unwanted kittens is a moral obligation of responsible pet owners. Neutering also reduces and eliminates sexually related problem behaviors.

KITTY NO-NO'S

We are so used to taking aspirin, ibuprofen and acetaminophen when we feel bad that it's tempting to give the same to our pets when they're feeling bad. But no matter how tempted, NEVER give your cat these medications. All are toxic to cats, even in one-pill doses. If you suspect your kitten has eaten these or other human medications, or any other kind of poison, call your veterinarian and the National Animal Poison Control Center (800-548-2423).

FEMALE PROBLEMS

It is during estrous, or heat, that female cats accept a mate and can become pregnant. Romantic girl cats loudly proclaim their desire, roll with abandon on the floor, and may even mark objects with urine to announce their availability to male Romeos. Heat behavior continues every two to three weeks during breeding season, from January to October. The behavior ends only when a cat becomes pregnant, the season ends, or she's spayed.

MALE PROBLEMS

Male cats may breed at any time after sexual maturity. Intact male cats aggressively mark their territory (the front door, the wall, your bed) with strong-smelling urine. If allowed outside, an unaltered male cat roams far from home and engages in ferocious fights with other boy cats. Cats are extremely prone to abscesses from scratch or bite wounds. Neutering dramatically reduces, and in some instances totally eliminates, objectionable spraying, fighting and roaming behavior, and the resulting battle wounds.

THE SURGERY

Because cats may become parents at as early as four months of age, the American Veterinary Medical Association now endorses neutering from sixteen weeks on. Some shelters provide the services as early as eight weeks of age. Young kittens bounce back from surgery more quickly than do older cats.

The surgeries are performed under general anesthetic, so your kitten doesn't feel any discomfort. A male cat's testicles are removed in surgery. This is called a gonadectomy, or castration. A female cat's ovaries and uterus are removed in surgery; this is called an ovariohysterectomy, or spay surgery.

The longest, thickest hairs on these kittens are called "guard hairs."

If you've not already done so, call your veterinarian NOW and schedule the operation. Neutering procedures are the most common elective surgeries veterinarians perform, and they are very safe when conducted by a veterinarian under sterile conditions. Altering may be a requirement of shelter adoptions, and agencies often offer reduced rates for the surgeries.

Emergencies and First Aid

Emergencies may require first aid, but you should always follow home care with immediate veterinary attention. Gently wrap your injured kitten in a thick towel to prevent her fighting you or further hurting herself. Place your ill or injured kitten in a box so that she can't see out, to calm her during the ride to the hospital.

A FIRST-AID KIT FOR CATS

Emergencies are the kinds of situations you hope never occur, but for which you should be most prepared. Keep the following items together, along with the name and phone number of your veterinarian and emergency clinic, so you can be prepared should your cat need emergency care.

adhesive tape

antibiotic ointment

blanket

cardboard box

cotton (balls, swabs, wrap)

hydrogen peroxide (3%)

oil (vegetable or mineral)

soap

thermometer (digital)

tweezers

washcloth

SHOCK

Signs of shock include being semi-conscious or unconscious, confusion and weakness, with rapid and/or shallow panting. Place your kitten on her side with head extended for easier breathing. You may need to open her mouth, and use a cloth to grip and gently pull out the tongue to help keep the airway open. Cover your kitten with the towel, but don't overheat her.

TRAUMA

Car accidents and falls can cause internal injuries or back trauma. Move your injured kitten as little as possible. Slide her onto a flat, rigid surface, like a cookie sheet or large clipboard. Then wrap a restraining towel loosely over her body and completely around the board. This will also keep simple broken bones from become more serious.

BLEEDING

Control bleeding by placing a gauze compress or clean washcloth directly on the wound and applying pressure. If the blood soaks through, don't change the cloth; simply place a second compress or washcloth over the first one, and continue applying the pressure.

BURNS

Apply cold water for five minutes to burns. If you're unable to immerse the burned area, soak a washcloth in ice water, wring it out, and lightly apply to the burned area. Treat chemical burns, like those caused by caustic household cleaners, by flushing with cool water for five minutes or longer.

RESPIRATORY DIFFICULTY

A kitten may stop breathing due to electrocution, drowning, strangulation or choking. If you suspect a foreign object and can readily see it when you open her mouth, you can try to remove it with tweezers. You should never pull string from your kitten's mouth; it may have a needle or fish hook on the end. Leave that one for your veterinarian.

DROWNING

For cases of drowning, grasp the kitten's hind legs with one hand and the nape of her neck with the other, and turn her upside down. Give her several brisk shakes or even several rapid downward swings, to help expel water from her lungs.

RESUSCITATION

If your kitten still doesn't breathe, place her on one side on a table or flat sturdy surface. Find the "elbow" of the front leg, and place your first three fingers flat on her side, behind the elbow. Press firmly, then release quickly; repeat every five seconds until she breathes on her own.

If the lungs are injured, you may need to breathe air into your kitten's lungs. Place her on her tummy, with her head in an upright position. Keeping her lips closed, place your lips over her nose and gently blow for two to three seconds. Repeat every two seconds.

Continue artificial respiration until your kitten begins breathing on her own. As long as her heart still beats (you'll feel the pulse on her side behind the left elbow), continue trying, even up to thirty minutes.

WHEN TO CALL YOUR VETERINARIAN

In any emergency situation, you should call your veterinarian immediately. You can make the difference in your kitten's life by staying as calm as possible when you call and by giving the doctor or assistant as much information as possible before you leave for the clinic. That way, your veterinarian will be able to take immediate, specific action to remedy your kitten's situation.

Emergencies include acute abdominal pain, suspected poisoning, burns, frostbite, dehydration, shock, abnormal vomiting or bleeding, and deep wounds. You should also consult your veterinarian if your kitten has a thick discharge from eyes or nose, is coughing or sneezing, refuses food, or has a change in bathroom habits. Never give your kitten human medication unless instructed to do so by your veterinarian.

You are the best judge of your kitten's health because you live with and observe her every day. If you notice changes—such as lethargy, which may indicate a fever caused by infection—don't hesitate to call your veterinarian. Normal cat temperature is 101–102.5 degrees; anything higher indicates illness.

TOPICAL POISON

The most common poisoning occurs from misapplication of flea products. Poisoned kittens salivate, tremble, act dazed, or may even lose consciousness. Signs can be immediate or occur several hours after the flea product application.

As soon as you see the signs, rinse your kitten with clear, cool water. Use a plain shampoo that doesn't have insecticide to wash the poison off. Then wrap your kitten in a towel and get her to the veterinarian.

OTHER POISONS

Your kitten's curiosity can get her in all kinds of trouble, and swallowing any number of common household products can poison her. Many human medications like aspirin and Tylenol are poisonous to cats; chocolate is also deadly; and certain houseplants can burn her mouth and make her sick.

Antifreeze tastes sweet but destroys kidney function if your kitten drinks it. Bug bites and stings can turn from itchy irritations to deadly reactions. Signs of toxicity vary depending on what Kitty gets into but may include diarrhea or vomiting, incoordination or convulsions, or trouble breathing.

Treatment also depends on the poison and ranges from inducing vomiting to feeding your kitten something to neutralize the agent. Unless you are very far from help, don't attempt home remedies, but simply get your poisoned pet to the veterinarian. Take the poison package and a sample of your kitten's vomit with you, to help the doctor determine the best treatment.

If you can't get help immediately, call your veterinarian or the National Animal Poison Control Center (800-548-2423) for guidance. Swallowing hydrogen peroxide induces vomiting, activated charcoal tablets help absorb certain poisons, and milk or lemon juice and water neutralizes various toxins. Keep some on hand for emergencies in case your veterinarian or the National Animal Poison Control Center suggests you use them.

Vomiting and Diarrhea
VOMITING

The first thing to recognize is the difference between vomiting and regurgitation.

Regurgitation is when the cat almost effortlessly expels undigested food. The food has only made it as far as the esophagus, so it will look similar to when it was chewed and swallowed, except that it will be coated in digestive juices.

Vomiting is the forceful expulsion of food from the stomach. It is preceded by retching, and the food appears at least partly digested.

Oddly, cats vomit more easily than other animals, and at times for no apparent reason. Mother cats vomit digested food for their kittens. Most vomiting is caused by swallowing something irritating to the stomach, like grass or hair, or by simply eating too fast. When a cat is about to vomit, he may pace, act restless, perhaps drool or try to swallow a lot, then his abdominal muscles will begin to contract, forcing the food up.

If your cat or kitten vomits and then recovers with no apparant side effects, chances are it's fine. Repetitious vomiting or vomiting accompanied by blood is cause for calling the veterinarian immediately.

DIARRHEA

Diarrhea is runny, unformed stool. This can be caused by dietary overload, in which case the colon can't keep up with the volume (very rare in kittens), or by eating something irritating to the intestines, which then whisk it through incompletely digested. Any number of things can cause this, from eating dead animals to rotten food to rich sauces to too much milk to swallowing a bead. Monitor the condition and consult with your veterinarian if it doesn't go away quickly or is accompanied by blood or other illness.

STATS FOR CATS

Here are tidbits of cat trivia with which you can impress cat lovers (and cats) at cocktail parties and the like. Did you know that . . .

The average weight of an adult male cat is 8.6 pounds, and of an adult female cat, 7.2 pounds.

The largest breed of cat is the Ragdoll. Males weigh 15 to 20 pounds.

The smallest breed of cat is the Singapura, which weighs from 4 to 6 pounds.

The cat has 40 more bones in its body than a human.

The cats Hellcat and Brownie were the sole heirs to the 415,000-acre estate of Dr. William Grier of San Diego when he died in 1963.

(From *The Quintessential Cat*, by Roberta Altman. New York: Macmillan, 1994.)

Your Kitten's Mental Health

Equally important to the sound growth of your kitten is his mental health. Kittens are curious creatures and can be quite social when they want to be. Don't leave your kitten alone for the entire day—at least until he's settled in and knows you and what to expect. Keep a supply of toys on hand. Try teaching some of the exercises in chapter 9. Enjoy your kitten!

Establish Good Habits

During the first year of life, proper medical care is critical to the long-term health and happiness of your new kitten. Kittens can become very sick very quickly from any number of common, potentially life-threatening cat disorders. Educating yourself to the potential health risks and taking appropriate preventive measures will help you enjoy that brand-new bundle of joy to her fullest potential, now and for years to come.

Enjoying

Your

part three

Kitten

chapter 8

Play and Learning

As you walk by, Kamikaze Kitten darts from beneath the sofa and grapples with your shoelaces. Then in an eyeblink, he's stalking imaginary prey, intent upon ambushing the malevolent creature stirring behind the drapes. But before he reaches his goal, something else distracts him. Now your kitten is bouncing through the room like a Muppet on springs.

Oh, what fun we have watching kittens play. As soon as they can wobble about on unsteady paws, they're bopping each other's ears and trying to catch their own (and Mom's) tail. But to your kitten, these games are more than furry fun.

Cats start playing at four weeks of age, and the games continue their whole life long. Play helps youngsters practice and develop the skills they'll need to be successful adults. Games also teach kittens important lessons about their world and promote physical and social development.

The Game of Life

Your kitten's senses are fully developed by about five weeks of age, but it takes longer to coordinate all those clumsy paws. Play helps develop the motor skills he'll use in everyday activities.

The first play behavior kittens practice is on their backs, belly up with paws waving in the air. As he grapples with that fluttering feather, he's also learning to coordinate claws and bites. This is a defensive pose adult cats use to bring all their claws into play.

Wrestling not only tones their muscles and perfects their biting and clawing techniques, it also teaches social skills. Youngsters learn proper feline etiquette and how to interact with siblings and adults like their mother. Exuberant kittens soon realize that claws hurt and that uninhibited bites on Mom's tail result in a hiss and a swat.

Your kitten's games are all variations of hunting, fighting and mating behaviors.

Every kitten game mimics an adult behavior used in hunting, fighting or mating. The sideways shuffle, back arched high as they tippy-toe around other kittens or objects, is used in defensive situations by adults.

Other play behavior includes the mouse pounce, bird swat, fish scoop, boxer stance and horizontal leaps. Games of tag or hide and seek echo the stalk, chase and pursuit used in hunting. Playing is also a fun way for your kitten to learn about objects. He discovers that a batting paw sends a ball or pencil rolling and bouncing across the floor, but that a bopped shoe just sits there. Play teaches him that a toy mouse stays put while he naps, but that a moth flutters away and hides. Games express kitty curiosity and provide an outlet for exploration.

Even more, play is a creative expression of your kitten's emotions. As your kitten grows up, he's very aware of the difference between play and serious business, even though the same skills are needed. Kittens and cats play because it's just plain fun.

Those who play together stay together.

Interactive Play

Playing with your kitten cements the bond of love and trust between you. Those who play together stay together. In effect, your kitten looks upon you as a "Super Cat" who supplies food, grooming and fun times, just like Mom-cat did.

Kittens want something to chase and capture that can be bitten and clawed and "killed." Your wiggling fingers are enticing, but don't encourage hand and finger games or your kitten will inevitably get in trouble when he draws blood. Besides, what's cute in a kitten becomes downright dangerous in a full-grown cat.

Variations of Toys

Light, easy-to-move-and-bite toys get raves from feline critics. Fishing-pole-style toys provide great interactive games. Movement that crosses his line of vision horizontally stimulates his chasing reaction more quickly than does movement directly away from him. Try rolling an object in front of your baby, and watch the fun. Some kittens even enjoy games of fetch.

Homemade toys are less expensive but provide just as much fun. An empty paper bag or box, a wad of crinkly paper, even the beam of the flashlight will delight your kitten. Try dropping a walnut inside an empty tissue box, and watch your kitten "fish."

Kittens often invent games that satisfy their curiosity. Cats learn to open cupboard doors, shred the hanging plant, and climb the drapes. Just as with any baby, play-time should be supervised.

The Sleepy Kitten

You may have noticed that Kitty likes napping almost as much as playing. Kittens need more rest than adults do, but even grownup cats sleep about sixteen hours every day. By the time Kitty is six years old, he will have spent only two years awake.

No one is sure why cats sleep so much. It may have to do with conserving energy so that awake time is spent in bursts of activity. In the wild, hunters who are extremely successful and catch mice quickly have more time to nap.

Kittens learn by watching and interacting with their mothers and littermates.

SLEEP CYCLES

Like human sleep, feline sleep is divided into stages of light and deep slumber. During the first month of life, kittens fall directly into deep sleep. Older kittens and adults alternate five or six minutes of deep sleep with fifteen to twenty minutes of light sleep. This stage allows your kitten to stay tuned in to scents and sounds, and spring quickly awake if something tweaks his interest.

During deep sleep, kitty muscles relax, he becomes hard to awaken, and feline dreams are born. Paws twitch, tails lash, and whiskers twitch, and he may mutter in his sleep as he stalks dream-prey. We humans dream for one and a half to two hours nightly, but your cat will dream up to three hours each day.

Whisker-Licking Clean

Your kitten's instinct to wash himself accomplishes more than just clean whiskers. Cats often groom when frightened, tense or hesitant about how to react to puzzling situations. Self-grooming may help the cat relieve tension and cope with conflict; the self-induced "kitty massage" seems to calm your kitten down.

Kittens love to play with lightweight, easy-to-move toys.

When your kitten is in conflict or a stressful situation, he may seem ready to react, but instead suddenly stops and starts grooming himself. For instance, if your kitten is caught in the act jumping up on the dining room table when he knows he shouldn't, he may stalk away with tail held high, then begin furiously grooming himself.

Mutual Grooming

Mutual grooming begins when kittens start licking and grooming each other and their mother at about three weeks of age. Mutual grooming focuses on hard-to-reach places like the head.

But mutual grooming is primarily a social gesture rather than a hygienic one. Family cats often indulge in mutual grooming sessions, and may purr and play with each other at the same time. Among cats, mutual grooming is a form of communication, sometimes an expression of love and companionship.

Cats extend this behavior to humans by licking us and accepting our petting. So when your kitten thinks enough of you to groom your hair, return the compliment. After all, the payment will be in whisker kisses and purrs.

Kitten Talk

A kitten's vocabulary is a combination of both verbal and nonverbal language. Understanding what Kitty's trying to say will help you avoid misunderstandings and improve your relationship with your cat.

Some cats, like Siamese, are more vocal than others, but every cat has something to say. More than sixteen different feline voice patterns have been identified, which are commonly divided in four categories: murmur patterns, vowel patterns, articulated sounds and strained intensity sounds.

PURRS AND TRILLS

Murmur patterns include purrs and trills. These are the happy sounds your kitten makes when he's feeling friendly and relaxed.

PURRS AND HISSES

Cats make some of the strangest noises; in fact, researchers have documented a range of 16 sounds specific to cats. The two most noticeable are purring and hissing, probably because both are done with gusto.

Purring is normally associated with pleasure, but cats also purr when they're injured or distressed. Purring is a primal response, and kittens start doing it when they're just a few days old. Purring increases in intensity as a cat's pleasure mounts.

What causes purring? When stimulated, the brain sends signals to muscles in the throat and vocal cords to vibrate. It is the action of these muscles that causes the purring sound—and sensation.

Hissing, on the other hand, is a clear signal from the cat to steer clear! It's a sound meant to scare an intruder. In the act of hissing, a jet of air, as well as spit and sound, is shot out through the cat's mouth. The question is, who hissed first, the cat or the snake?

Purrs range from quiet, almost silent vibrations, to reverberating rumbles that nearly rattle the window-panes. Trills express joy when Kitty's bowl is filled or when you bring out a favorite toy.

MEOWS

The scent glands all over kittens help them mark their territory and companions.

Vowel patterns, like meows, are feline demands for *something*. Meows vary from short, muted mews to raucous, multisyllabic cat calls. Kittens meow to Mom-cat, but otherwise meows seem aimed primarily at humans. Higher pitches generally have a more pleasant connotation, while the lower tones tend to indicate more agitation. Your kitten typically meows to be petted, for attention or more food, and (if it's allowed) to go in and out.

CHIRPS

Articulated sounds like chirping and chattering usually indicate frustration. If you hear your kitten chittering, chances are he's seen something he can't reach—like a squirrel out the window.

SPITS AND SCREAMS

Strained intensity sounds are used in mating, offense, and defense. A frightened kitten may hiss and spit; an angry kitten may growl; and a defensive kitten howls, yowls, and finally, screams.

Marking Behavior

Cats communicate with smells as well as sounds, and they use specialized scent glands to mark their belongings. Scent glands in your kitten's lips, chin, forehead, tail, and between his toes release a personal scent when he rubs against or scratches an object.

Friendly cats first sniff each other's nose, then tail; don't be offended if your kitten presents his tail for you to sniff as a token of friendship. Your kitten leaves a scent mark every time he winds himself about your ankles, rubs your cheek, and bumps your forehead. Head butting is a particularly friendly greeting used between feline friends—an expression of affection. When your kitten rubs against you, he's marking you as his very own personal property . . . quite a compliment!

Cats typically forge a strong attachment to place. Personal kitty property includes his house, the view of the yard and, of course, his owner. In multiple cat homes, each cat often "owns" a particular part of the house, like the upstairs or downstairs, or a certain piece of furniture. Interlopers are warned off by both the scent and visual signs that your kitten leaves behind.

Unaltered adult cats often spray urine to mark territory, which can be decidedly unpleasant when indoors. They back up to objects with their tail straight up, tip quivering, and release strong-smelling urine in short bursts. Altering nearly always eliminates spraying and reduces the strong tomcat urine odor to a bearable level.

Body Language

Most cat language is nonverbal. Body language is second nature to cats, who are extremely visual animals. Experts speculate that silent "felinese" developed in wild cats as a way to communicate without alerting enemies or prey to their presence. Your kitten speaks volumes using tail twitches, ear flicks, eye winks and even fur and body positions.

TAILS

The tail is probably the best communicator Kitty has, and is a good indicator of his mood. An upright tail belongs to a confident cat checking his surroundings. An upright tail with a hook on the end is a friendly greeting to older cats and humans.

A tail in a relaxed horizontal position indicates a mellow mood, while a slightly curved and raised tail shows interest. But if your kitten reverses that curve so that his tail becomes an arch, he's feeling threatened.

A wagging tail expresses aggravation. A twitch or two of the tip is a warning, which soon escalates to thumps and then full lashing. A flailing tail says, "Lay off!" If you ignore the warning, Kitty will land an angry claw swipe, or worse.

EYES

Feline eyes are windows to your kitten's soul. Curious, alert kittens are wide-eyed so that they won't miss a thing. Unblinking stares or slitted eyes are signs of aggression. Relaxed, trusting kittens let their eyelids droop as though sleepy.

Sudden emotion of any kind, from joy to fear or anger, is shown by sudden dilation of the eyes. Abrupt contraction of the pupils to a slit can warn of an imminent attack.

Curious, alert kittens are wide-eyed and prick-eared.

EARS

Kitten ears are equally expressive. When the ears are upright and the face forward to catch every sound, Kitty's interested and alert. Uneasy ears turn sideways like little airplane wings. Scaredy-cats press their ears flat to the side of the head. The more the back of the ear shows, the readier the cat is to attack.

FUR AND WHISKERS

Even your kitten's fur signals mood and intention. Forward-facing whiskers mean he's alert and checking things out. Spread whiskers show Kitty's happy and relaxed, but whiskers flatten against cheeks when he's fearful or plans to attack. Kittens aroused by strong emotion, such as fear or even play, fluff their fur and bristle their tail.

BODY POSITION

Body position is a form of long-distance communication that can be seen from afar. A contented kitten typically sits on his haunches with his tail wrapped about himself. Dropping into a curtsy with front feet lowered and tail end raised, or rolling on the ground in front of you, is an invitation to play.

Confident kittens face threats head-on, while the uneasy kitten crouches with front paws drawn close to his chest. A fearful kitten turns into a Halloween cat, arching his back sideways to the enemy in order to look bigger and more impressive.

Your kitten's body language will tell you how he's feeling—like "inquisitive!"

HIERARCHY

The feline chain of command is despotic. Rather than a stair-step ranking, the kitty hierarchy tends to have one ruler, with the rest ranking somewhere below. The high-ranking feline usually holds claim to the most territory, and/or has been around the longest. Normally, youngsters give way to senior cats, and altered cats bow to intact felines.

FELINE ACTORS

Despite all the bristled fur, flailing tails and hissing contests, cats are not great attackers. They're simply brilliant at posturing, and they use felinese to fake out their opponents without ever mussing a whisker.

A fearful cat bluffs his foe by trying to look bigger than he really is. He fluffs his fur and turns broadside, and he tippy-toes sideways away from the threat, pressing his ears lower and lower. He spits and snarls and may try to warn away with a claw swipe. But if the enemy isn't impressed, he admits defeat and runs.

Even confident cats first try to frighten interlopers away. If a head-on, wide-eyed stare doesn't work, his ears turn to the side, his tail starts swinging, and he bares his teeth and lowers his head. Unless the intruder takes to his heels, a cat on the offensive will attack with tooth and claw.

Although cats do occasionally indulge in pitched battles, most avoid conflict by acting tougher than they really are. Posturing displays may go on for twenty minutes or longer, with both cats indulging in dancelike maneuvering involving fluffed fur and ferocious expressions and vocalizations. The victory belongs to the most dominant kitty, who doesn't lose face and slink away.

chapter 9

Basic
Training

"Train a cat?" you say. "Surely, you jest!"

Actually, cats are extremely intelligent and learn very easily when something interests them. For instance, kittens quickly learn where their food is stored and how to open the cupboard door.

But unlike dogs, whose pack mentality prompts them to please humans, cats rarely relish obedience to another. In fact,

cats train humans to believe they're untrainable so that owners don't expect good behavior from them. But if your kitten is to be a welcome member of your family, she must learn a few simple rules.

Rules to Remember

First, correcting bad behavior after the fact will only confuse your cat. She won't understand she's being punished for shredding the

113

newspaper if it happened hours ago. *Corrections are effective only when you catch Kitty in the act.*

Second, cats do not respond well to physical correction. Slapping or hitting simply makes Kitty fear your hands, something she'll remember the next time you want to pet her. It can also make aggressive cats strike back and become more aggressive, while irreparably traumatizing shy kittens.

THE "NO" MESSAGE

Verbal chastisement sometimes works, particularly with kittens. If you're fortunate, a kitten's obedience to Mom-cat may be transferred to you. But don't shout at your cat; instead use an authoritative "No!" in response to poor behavior. Many kittens understand your meaning if you hiss at them, "SSSSSSST!" like Mom-cat did to signal inappropriate behavior.

Don't chuckle or smile when you chastise, or Kitty will know you're more amused than aggravated. Be consistent: Don't let her do something one day, then scold her for it the next; changing the rules is confusing. Don't dwell on negatives, or she will learn that breaking rules is the best way to get attention, even if it's negative.

THE "YES" MESSAGE

Instead, reward good behavior with effusive praise. Talk to your kitten and tell her what a smart, wonderful cat she is, and why. Most cats learn to understand many human words, and the more they know, the fewer misunderstandings and opportunities for misbehavior there will be.

The easiest way to train a cat is to make the desired behavior more fun than the alternative. Cats respond best to positive reinforcement like treats, playtime and owner attention.

Finally, when correction is necessary, don't let Kitty know it came from you. To your cat, you are the source of comfort, love, good food and fun times. Negative reinforcement should seem to arise from the "unknown," the Almighty Invisible Paw of the Cat-God. Otherwise, Kitty will behave only when you're in the vicinity and ignore the rules when you're out of range.

Booby traps, long-distance squirt guns, loud noises and other harmless unpleasantness persuade Kitty it's really not so much fun after all to leap on the counter, swing from the tablecloth or scratch the sofa. See chapter 10 for more information.

Using the Litter Box

By about three weeks of age, kittens begin imitating Mom. They taste and mouth her food, lick themselves and each other, and follow her to the litter box. With few exceptions, kittens will already know what litter is for by following Mom-cat's example.

By imitating mom, and because they're so clean, kittens train themselves to use the litter box.

Some kittens will need a little help in the potty department, though. Just like with buying a house, the three most important issues in litter box training are location, location, location. Even if the kitten understands what to do with litter, you must make sure she knows where the box is and that she can get to it in time. The litter box should be convenient for her to use but some

115

distance from eating and sleeping areas, or you'll offend her sense of kitty decorum. A low-traffic area that provides some privacy is perfect.

Keep about two inches of clean litter in the box. Cats like monotony, so once you've found an acceptable litter, don't switch brands unless you must. Sudden change may upset your kitten and disrupt bathroom habits, and then neither of you will be happy.

ENCOURAGE GOOD HABITS

Right after a meal, a potty break is often imminent. The first few times, either set your kitten on the litter or let her climb in by herself. Encourage Kitty to scratch and sniff about by digging in the litter with your finger. She should quickly get the right idea. Wait until she finishes, then offer lots of verbal praise. It's important that the litter box remain clean, but for the first week or so, leave your kitten's freshest deposit behind as a fragrant reminder. Let her follow you away from the box so that she'll learn its location. Soon, she'll follow you to the box after each meal or head off for a private session on her own when she feels the need.

Each cat has her own bathroom etiquette, and you may discover Kitty likes privacy and accomplishes more if you don't watch. And don't be concerned if your kitten's excavation technique seems odd. Some cats dig a hole first, make their deposit, then cover it up, while others are content to leave contributions on the surface. Enthusiastic diggers who tunnel as though heading for China may need a covered pan to keep from emptying the litter onto the floor. Others may only go through the motions of covering their waste.

Leaving waste uncovered is a sign of dominance, but most cats bury their deposits in deference to the Super-Cat person with whom they live. As long as Kitty hits the box, be happy.

Clawing Conduct

Clawing is normal feline behavior, and you cannot, nor should you, train the behavior away. The trick is to redirect needle-sharp kitty claws away from your furniture and give Kitty another, better scratching outlet.

Place the scratching post in a convenient area near her bed or food bowl (cats enjoy a good scratch after eating or sleeping). If it's stuck away in the corner of an empty room, don't expect her to hunt it down; she'd rather stay with you and use your footstool.

MAKE IT A GAME

To begin, make scratching a game. Direct your kitten's attention to the post, using a peacock feather or another irresistible kitten toy. Tease her with the fluttering feather all around the scratching post, playing hide and seek. Your kitten will naturally grab the post as she tries to catch the feather. Demonstrate what you want and scratch it yourself; then praise when she scratches.

Whenever you catch your kitten flexing claws somewhere she shouldn't, hiss or tell her "No!" and gently move her to the post. Your kitten may get the idea faster if a vertical post is set on its side so that she can actually sit on the post and dig in.

Older kittens who have already developed bad habits may need stronger correction. Remember, the cat isn't stupid, she knows she shouldn't scratch the sofa, because you've told her so. But like a three-year-old child, Kitty often tests your will, in effect saying, "I know you said 'no' before, but that was two minutes ago, and maybe you changed your mind!" Such sneaky cats are angels while you're present, then turn into imps when you're away.

ENFORCING THE MESSAGE

All's fair in fooling the feline: Long-distance correction is the most effective tool. Do not acknowledge the bad behavior in any way; act as though you're dumber than a rock and don't know what's going on. Surreptitiously use a spray bottle adjusted to a thin stream, and squirt the miscreant on the heinie. Again, don't react—this should be perceived by your cat as an Act of the Cat God. You don't want to soak your kitten, just startle her out of the behavior.

Always praise your kitten when she chooses the correct scratching apparatus. With some consistency, Kitty will learn what prompts praise and what results in a wet tail.

Though cats may be aloof by nature, they're easily enticed to play.

Treating the post with catnip will attract most adult cats but not kittens. Catnip is an acquired taste that comes with maturity, and even then, not all cats react to it.

Lining the Cat Carrier

All cats must travel from time to time, and often they view carriers as the prelude to an unpleasant visit to the veterinarian or groomer. As soon as the carrier appears, cats become invisible. They must be pulled kicking and screaming from hidy-holes, and only with the greatest difficulty inserted into the carrier for the trip. Cats seem to view the carrier as a monster that swallows them up and carts them away.

It doesn't have to be that way. Cats are drawn to cave-like spaces in which to sleep and play. Make the carrier a natural part of the furniture, not stuck away on some shelf. Leave the door open so that your kitten can discover and investigate it at her leisure.

Try tossing a Ping-Pong ball into a hard-sided carrier. Kitty will have a wonderful time chasing it around. Or put a favorite toy or bedding inside or on top of the carrier. Left to her own devices, Kitty may choose the carrier as a preferred sleeping nest.

As your kitten becomes more accustomed to the crate, occasionally close the door for short periods, then release her. Once she's comfortable with the door closed, carry her about in the house, and eventually take her for short car rides around the block. Don't make her only experiences in the carrier end at the vet's.

Walking on Leash

Even those who have never had a dog identify leash training in distinctly doggy terms. Throw those thoughts out of your head. Although cats are perfectly capable of walking on a leash, they are not content to be tugged into a proper heel position or gaited about at an unbecoming clip.

LET THEM LEAD

Cats tend to tolerate and even relish leash walks when they lead the way. They stroll and will not be rushed, indulging in a sniff here and a pause there, investigating a dragonfly or the rustle of mousy interlopers. Trying to force a faster pace generally results in Kitty putting on the brakes. Cats quite literally stop to smell the roses . . . and the sidewalk, your shoe, the leaves . . .

START YOUNG

Much patience is necessary to acclimatize the cat to the whole idea of harnesses and leads, and kittenhood is the perfect time to learn. Leash training gives your cat the pleasure of safely supervised outdoor excursions. For health reasons, however, you should wait to go outside until your kitten has had all her shots.

Leash training isn't for all cats, nor is the outdoors. Some are perfectly content to keep carpet beneath their paws their whole life long and are terrified without a roof between them and the sky.

An invaluable tool used by trainers of animal actors is a simple handheld clicker, often available around Halloween. The clicker is used in combination with bits of canned cat food (tiny pieces!) that Kitty particularly likes. The sound reinforces and signals that she's done something right. She does not have to be hungry to respond, so don't think you have to deny her dinner.

TRAIN SLOWLY

All initial training takes place in the safety of your house. First, just as you did with the carrier, leave the leash and harness out for Kitty to investigate on her own. After she's thoroughly sniffed it, rubbed it, and decided it's no threat, you're ready for the next step: donning the equipment.

This is a big deal for cats. Have your treats ready, then put the harness on your kitten. Don't bother yet with the leash. If you're fortunate, she will consider the halter a wonderful new game, and it won't slow her down. But many cats roll and meow in distress, trying to scrape the harness off.

In either case, tempt Kitty to walk by waving the treat under her nose. When she stands and walks with the harness on, praise her, click the clicker, and give her the treat. You should give the click and treat simultaneously, but only as a reward for performing correctly. Give Kitty the click-treat each time she walks to you, but do not give a click-treat unless she stands up and walks.

ADDING THE LEASH

Leave the harness on for ten minutes, two to three times a day. Again, reward with a click-treat only when Kitty walks while wearing it. When she appears comfortable with the harness, simply attach the leash and let her drag it about the room. She may revert to rolling, or it may not faze her at all. As before, reward her when she's vertical and moving.

Then pick up the end of the leash. Loop the end securely about one hand, and control the slack with the other. Give her roaming room, but offer a gentle tug now and again to guide her. When she responds to the tug and follows your direction, give her a click-treat reward. Repeat the exercise for short periods two to three times a day until Kitty is comfortable.

The outdoors will be a place to explore together once your kitten is harness- and leash-trained.

OUT YOU GO!

Finally, if your kitten is old enough (at least sixteen weeks old) and has had all protective shots, you're ready for the outdoors. Walk the route first by yourself so that you can avoid barking dogs, heavy traffic or other hazards. Choose a quiet park or your backyard for your strolls. Slowly phase out click-treat rewards, for soon Kitty will be walking and sniffing, listening and watching for the pure pleasure alone.

Coming When Called

Yes, cats can be trained to come when called. This can be particularly helpful when you need to find your cat quickly. And if you've had your kitten any length of time, you know there's one sure-fire thing that brings her running. Food.

Were cats not safely confined to their individual houses, the sound of the can opener would bring them running from miles away. Use that simple principle, coupled with click-treat rewards, to bring your kitten running at other times as well.

As you prepare her meal and she's running to you, call her name, saying, "Kitty, come!" When she arrives, give her a click-treat and set down the food. Do this every time she's fed, and soon she'll relate her name being called with a food reward. The clicker lets her know she's done what you wanted.

Then try calling her at other than mealtimes. When she comes running, have the click-treat ready. Make it a game, crossing to the other side of the room or hiding behind a chair, calling, "Kitty, come!" and having her come to different locations to receive a click-treat.

Once she's coming consistently, you'll want to phase out the click-treats and reward her only occasionally. Intermittent reinforcement is a much more powerful training tool: Because she never knows when she'll get rewarded, she tries every time.

Tricks

Soon you will read how to train your kitty to do some basic tricks. To encourage you and help you feel you're not crazy in this endeavor, we've included this excerpt from Roberta Altman's *The Quintessential Cat* (New York: Macmillan, 1994). It tells you how people through the centuries have trained their cats.

"In the nineteenth century, Pietro Capelli gained an international reputation with his troupe of performing cats. As a boy growing up in Italy, he was too poor to have pets, but he loved cats. And when his friends were playing games in the street, Pietro was at the local dump hanging out with the cats. He watched them play and work and scrounge for food. He helped cats who were hurt and would give up his own food so that his cats would not go hungry. One day he decided to see if he could train his cats and started teaching them simple tricks." Soon he was putting on shows for kids in the neighborhood. Word spread and adults began showing up as well. Capelli ended up rich and famous, with his cats swinging from trapeze, balancing on high wires, and lying on their backs and juggling with their hind legs. He taught them to prepare rice using a mortar and pestle, play children's instruments, and draw water from a well, obtaining the number of buckets that he called for.

"The Englishman Leoni Clarke had a troupe of fifty trained cats who could walk across a stage on tightropes, jump through flaming hoops, and parachute down from the ceiling. He called himself The King of the Cats. And of course today, many cats have been trained to star in commercials and films."

Trick Training

As mentioned before, cats do not appreciate physical correction. With a dog, the trainer physically positions him into a sit by pushing on his hips. Do that with a cat and she'll look at you in disbelief, then stalk off in disgust.

Cats also don't understand why they should do what you want just because they love you. The click-treat is a very convincing argument that most cats seem to understand. In fact, the click-treat technique can train all kinds of behaviors, like sitting, by building on the cat's own natural movement.

Sit   For a sit, hold the treat in front of the standing cat's face and slowly move the treat up. When Kitty sits in response, click the clicker and give her the treat.

Beg   To teach her to beg, hold the treat near her nose while she's sitting, and then move it up and just above her head. To follow the reward, she'll sit up and beg. Give her the click-treat.

Lie Down   To train your kitten to lie down, set her on a table and move the treat in front of her face slowly, down and below table level. Her face will follow the treat, and her body will drop down. Couple these hand signals with trigger words like "sit" or "down," and eventually you'll amaze friends with your genius cat.

Again, much patience is needed, and every cat is different. Experiment with what prompts your kitten to do certain things. Does she paw the air when you flick a feather? Give her a click-treat to reinforce the behavior, and she's learned to wave. Does she leap from chair-back to shoulder when you dangle a toy? Or will she play fetch with crumpled paper balls? Amazing trick training results when you simply reward your kitten's natural behavior.

chapter 10

Acting Up

Nearly all bad behavior on the part of your kitten can be traced to misunderstanding: Something gets lost in the translation from felinese to English, resulting in a recalcitrant cat and a disgruntled owner.

Though it may seem so, your kitten doesn't act up out of vindictiveness. Most behaviors, even bad ones, make perfect sense to Kitty. Sometimes your kitten is simply acting like a normal cat, while other times he's trying to tell you something. Feline behavior problems can get very complicated. It all comes down to how you interpret Kitty's unusual antics—or, worse, aggressions. You must become a detective to ferret out the reason behind the poor behavior, and try to correct it.

Common Problems

The most common feline behavior complaints are:

- Inappropriate scratching
- Hit-or-miss bathroom habits
- Excessive shyness
- Aggression

Any one or combination of these can be provoked by three main things. First, kittens act up when they don't understand what's expected—or they're not offered a better alternative. Second, problem behaviors can stem from stress. Third, discomfort or illness may prompt inappropriate behaviors.

To stop problem behaviors, learn what your kitten needs so that you're offering him appropriate alternatives. Learn what causes stress so that you can eliminate or buffer the causes. And learn what normal healthy behavior is like so that you can recognize sick kitty behavior and get him help. Stress can be caused by many things, including illness, but a major factor with cats is change.

Cats bond to the place where they live and are extremely territorial; therefore, they are sensitive to any kind of change in the household. Moving upsets many cats, but some kitties react to something as simple as changing the drapes or rearranging the furniture. A new baby, pet or spouse in the house can be quite upsetting (see chapter 11 for more on this subject). Some cats take things in stride, but for most, change must be gradual to avoid minor to severe behavior problems.

Crime and Punishment

Again, corporal punishment does not work with cats. Behavior-modification techniques, however, may be beneficial: One lets Kitty know that his undesirable behavior has unpleasant consequences, so he chooses to be good. You interrupt the behavior, then offer Kitty a more appealing alternative.

Different things work with different cats. A long-distance squirt gun or plant spray bottle is effective for some. Short bursts of water (never in the face!) work best. Other cats respond better to a shaker can filled with coins or marbles, or even a pillow tossed toward them. Shy cats may become frightened if the noise is too loud, while hard-case cats may need a foghorn to break their concentration.

KITTY DETERRENTS

Booby traps work well for kittens who misbehave only when you're out of sight. Setting out tin foil, double-sided tape or a plastic floor runner (nub side up) will repel many counter-climbing kitties from off-limits areas. Try stacking empty soda cans on the counter, or balance one on the toilet paper roll so that it falls off when Kitty leaps up or tries to shred the bathroom tissue.

Set mousetraps upside down so that they won't catch his paws but will only bounce and snap to startle him away. Sprinkle cayenne pepper, onion powder or citrus scent to repel curious cats from garbage cans, plants and other items.

Kittens and cats are easily upset by changes—even moving furniture.

The key to successful behavior modification is consistency. Kitty should face the consequences every time, and at the very moment, he indulges in bad behavior. If you can't be there to catch him, kitten-proof a "safe room" with his litter box, bowls and toys, and isolate him there when you're out until you can trust him.

Litter Box Woes

First of all, spraying behavior is different than indiscriminate urination. Spraying cats—generally, older intact males—use urine to mark property. The target is almost always a vertical surface, like the wall or one side of the furniture. Neutering usually eliminates this problem.

But marking behavior can be triggered by stress in an anxious kitten who's more on the fearful side. The stress of seeing a strange cat walk across the lawn, or having an unexpected houseguest, may trigger scent marking. Kitty's trying to feel more comfortable by spreading his scent. He may use lots of chin and head rubbing, or even spraying, to mark the visitor's suitcase or even your belongings, to declare his ownership of you. He may become so stressed that he starts rejecting his litter box completely.

Sprinkling cayenne pepper on the ground may deter your kitten from playing with your plants.

Indiscriminate urination is simply elimination outside of the litter box. Always consider health problems as a possible culprit, and have your veterinarian check your cat.

If your kitten is hanging over the edge and dropping his deposits outside the box, chances are you simply need a larger pan. Covered facilities will keep him from letting it all hang out.

Kittens who have been declawed have tender paws and may refuse boxes with rough litter. Your veterinarian will recommend alternatives (like shredded newspaper) until Kitty's paws heal.

CLEANLINESS IS KEY

More commonly, a kitten may simply reject a dirty litter box. Keep the box clean, or he may find another place to potty . . . like your carpet. He wants to step into a dry box, so scoop out the solid waste and wet spots daily. Set a schedule to clean the box thoroughly: Change the litter completely, and scrub out the pan.

Different litters last longer than others, but weekly cleaning is a good guide. If more than one cat uses the box, you may need to clean more often. Use a mild detergent and warm water, and rinse thoroughly; cats reject the litter box if it smells too strongly of disinfectant or powerful deodorants. Some cats demand their own private toilets, so you may need to provide a box for each one.

LOCATION, LOCATION . . .

A poor litter box location is another reason for missing the mark. First, be sure your kitten knows where the box is. Kittens may not be able to get there in time if the box is placed in an out-of-the-way place. If the litter box is too close to sleeping or eating areas, your kitten may refuse to use the box. Once you've established his potty place, don't move the box around. Cats don't like change, and relocating the bathroom isn't playing fair and can create indiscriminate elimination problems.

Changing litter brands can also make Kitty boycott the box. Most cats accept clay-type litters that have a sandy texture, but many reject those with strong scents. Once you've found a litter your kitten likes, stick with it. If you absolutely must change brands, do so gradually, first mixing one-third of the new in with two-thirds of the old, and gradually increasing the percentage until you've switched.

ACCIDENTS

Be sure to clean your kitten's "accidents" with an odor neutralizer, available at most pet supply stores. Otherwise, the scent may prompt your kitten to return to the scene of the crime and become a repeat offender. Try spritzing on a little citrus scent to make the spot less attractive.

Kittens do the darndest things!

Feed Kitty right on the dirty spot, and he'll stop eliminating there. Leave the empty bowl behind as a reminder. After a week, take the bowl away for a day, then replace it. Do this every-other-day routine for a week, then gradually move the bowl back to the right place. If he's messing in several spots, plastic carpet runners placed nub side up will help.

If you've got a hard-case cat who insists on using the living room rug, some behavior modification is in order. Remember, to make him understand that his behavior has unpleasant consequences, zap him in the act. Then move him to the litter box, and praise him when he eliminates in the right spot.

Scratching Solutions

Cats most often scratch in inappropriate places because their scratching post isn't adequate for their needs. If it isn't the right texture or height, or in the right location, Kitty will find something that is.

Don't allow your kitten to scratch an old chair or sofa. He won't understand why you've changed the rules when new furniture is bought. Remember that scratching is a form of territorial marking that is also physically and emotionally beneficial. And the longer he scratches something, the harder it will be to change his mind, since his scent will be etched into the object.

Take a minute, and watch to see exactly what your kitten *is* scratching. Is it the back of an armchair? the door frame? or the woven seat of Grandma's antique rocking chair? Pay attention to what he is scratching, and you will be able to do better at selecting a post that he will want to scratch.

Perhaps you've listened to your kitten and bought him the perfect post, but he still won't use it. Be sure that the scratching object is easily accessible to the cat, that he doesn't have to hunt to find it. Kitty would much rather stay in the living room with you to do his scratching. (See chapter 9 for advice on post location.)

LESSENING THE APPEAL

Use furniture shampoo to clean your kitten's favorite upholstered targets (usually the corners). Removing or dulling the scent can make the object less attractive. Cat-repellent sprays, which may also help, are available from pet supply stores. Firmly attaching plastic covers to targeted furniture also dissuades some cats. And if you've determined the scratching/marking behavior results from stress, removing the anxiety can reduce excessive scratching.

Finally, use behavior modification to make things uncomfortable for your kitten whenever he scratches the wrong thing. Zap him with a stream of water, blow a whistle, or shake a coffee can filled with marbles to distract him from the behavior. Then scoop him up and show him where it's okay to scratch.

If Kitty's dead-set on scratching the sofa, cover the injured areas with plastic and set the scratching post right in front. Once your kitten finally makes the connection in his kitty brain and starts scratching the right object, you can slowly move the scratching post to a more permanent position.

The key to eliminating inappropriate scratching is to make it unpleasant for the cat *and* offer a better solution. You *can* do this—and have nice furniture, too!

Phrases

This passage is excerpted from The Quintessential Cat, *by Roberta Altman (New York: Macmillan, 1994).*

The cat has entered our language in a number of colorful phrases. Though you may recognize many of them, and have used them at one time or another, do you know their origin? Here are some common cat phrases and how they evolved:

It's raining cats and dogs: This expression originated several centuries ago when streets in cities and towns were narrow, dirty and poorly drained. When there was a heavy rain, large numbers of starving cats and dogs would simply drown. When the rain ended, people would find the bodies of the dead cats and dogs in the streets. Some of the people thought the bodies of the animals fell with the rain, hence they said it rained "cats and dogs." In another explanation, the expression originated in Norse mythology, where cats symbolize heavy rain and dogs represent great gusts of wind. The phrase is also a slang term for highly speculative, low-priced securities or for a large, odd assortment of goods for sale; and it may be used in reference to the violence associated with fights between cats and dogs—perhaps best summed up in this quote from "The Duel," written by the American journalist and poet Eugene Field:

> *The Gingham dog went "Bow-wow-wow!"*
> *And the Calico cat replied "Mee-ow!"*
> *The air was littered, an hour or so,*
> *With bits of gingham and calico.*

Letting the cat out of the bag: This phrase, now used when someone has revealed a secret, dates back to a scam practiced on market day in the eighteenth century. Piglets were often taken to market in a bag, and since a cat was worth much less than a piglet, a dishonest farmer would put a cat in the bag instead of a piglet. If the potential buyer wanted to see the piglet before paying for it, he would be told that the piglet was too feisty and it was too risky to open the bag as he might run away. However, if meows started coming from the bag, or the cat struggled so much that the seller had to let it out, his secret became common knowledge. He had, therefore, let the cat out of the bag.

Having kittens: This phrase refers to a state of great upset or anxiety. The source of this phrase goes back to medieval times, when cats were thought of as witches' familiars. If a pregnant woman was suffering agonizing pain, it was believed that she was bewitched and the pain was caused by the kittens inside her womb scratching and struggling to get out. Since witches have supernatural powers, they could supply magical potions to destroy the litter so that the woman would not give birth to kittens. As late as the seventeenth century, "cats in the belly" was an accepted excuse in court for getting an abortion. It does not seem unlikely that a woman who thought she was bewitched and going to give birth to kittens would become hysterical with fear—hence the phrase "having kittens."

Curiosity killed the cat: Originally this phrase was "care killed the cat," which related to the fact that a cat has nine lives and that "care will wear them out." A woman who is spiteful and backbiting is often referred to as a cat, that woman is frequently thought of as being nosy or curious, and thus evolved the phrase "curiosity killed the cat."

Looks like the cat who's swallowed the canary: This expression is used to describe a person who "looks" guilty, although I'm not so sure any cat feels guilt after such an act. It's an American phrase that dates back to the 1870s.

Shrinking Violets

Shy kitties can react to stress by becoming withdrawn and depressed, and may hide or stop eating when faced with unexpected change. It's much easier to try to prevent shyness and boost confidence during kittenhood than to deal with depression later.

The socialization period in kittens occurs between two and seven weeks of age. During this time, your kitten learns who is friend and foe, and how to react in various situations. If the baby led a very sheltered life, or if Mom-cat reacted negatively to certain things, then the kitten may have become shy of those same experiences.

By exposing your kitten to a variety of nonthreatening events at an early age, you'll help Kitty gain confidence and be less spooked by the unusual. Perhaps he's fine with you but is terrified of other men, women, children or pets. Maybe loud noises like thunder bother him. Desensitization is possible—the procedure of exposing timid cats to upsetting events in small doses. But often, extreme shyness in adult cats requires professional help.

Playing interactive games is the best (and most fun) way to promote confidence in a shrinking-violet cat. Drag a string or toy for your kitten to stalk and pounce, and let him win and capture the prey. Fishing-pole-style toys are excellent for building confidence.

Playing Rough

The most common problem with aggression in kittens is play behavior. Kitty isn't trying to be mean; he's just using his cat-given gifts to have fun. But even kitten teeth and claws hurt.

First of all, never let the kitten use your hand as a toy. If your kitten does bite or claw you, pulling away triggers a reaction to hold on even harder. Instead, pushing *toward* him will induce Kitty to release you. Try saying "Sssssst!" or a similar trigger word in a high-pitched voice each time this happens so that Kitty associates the trigger word with letting go. In time, you should be able to prevent oncoming attacks simply by saying the trigger word before contact is made.

If Kitty pounces and grabs your ankles when you're moving, he's probably play-hunting. Anticipate attacks, and have a better toy ready to toss and distract him. You may need to carry your squirt gun or some other gentle reminder to stop play attacks.

Some aggressive kitties become very vocal to get their way. Rewarding copious meows with food and/or attention reinforces the behavior. Constant meows can indicate pain, but more often they're demands. To mute the meows, ignore Kitty when he's noisy and only pay attention (feed and play with him) when he's quiet. You may need the spray bottle to make your point.

Let your cat know if he's playing too rough by stopping the game.

Also, pay attention to your kitten's silent language. Aggression almost never occurs without warning. Watch his eyes, ears and tail for clues that Kitty is peeved, and try to understand what's causing his ire. Perhaps he's feeling cornered or isn't in the mood for petting. Maybe he just saw a squirrel outside stomping on his lawn, and his pent-up kitten rage needs an outlet.

Other times, your kitten will use nonverbal aggression to get his way. If you pick him up every time he grabs your ankle, you've also reinforced the behavior. When he learns that snarling and biting stops the child next door from pulling his tail, he may become aggressive if faced with any child.

Again, avoid rewarding the behavior. Don't pick him up, don't play with him, and don't give him attention for aggressive behavior. The only thing his biting and clawing should produce is a squirt from your spray bottle.

Watching Kitty's body langauge will help you know what he's up to.

Ask for Help

Aggression in adult cats can be very complicated, particularly in multiple cat homes. It can result from territorial disputes, frightening changes in the household, stress, illness and even pain. Veterinarians and feline behaviorists or therapists are in the best position to help owners of aggressive or extremely shy cats.

chapter 11

Introducing
Your Kitten to
Strangers

Change is a part of life humans take for granted. But cats dislike the unexpected. Even minor variations can be upsetting, and new people or pets can really get Kitty's whiskers in a twist.

The key to any change is to take your time. Introductions that are too rapid can result in behavior problems. Confident cats can become aggressive, while shy kitties may withdraw into depression.

The younger your kitten is when meeting strangers, the more accepting of them she will be. Acquiring two kittens at the same time is easier than buying two at different times, and introducing kittens to adults is simpler than introducing two adults to each other. If you plan on getting a dog, borrow a friendly pooch and introduce Kitty to the wonderful world of canines in advance.

Planning a family? Make sure your kitten is introduced to young children now. Expose her to a number of people so that she understands that other men, women, and children are the same species as you. At the very least, cats should be able to meet your veterinarian without having a hissy fit. Single cat owners who anticipate marriage should acclimatize their kitten to members of the opposite sex. An irate spraying cat tends to put a damper on romance.

Who Asked for Another Cat!?

Although some cats appreciate a feline buddy, others relish being only cats. She's used to having your undivided attention and the run of the house. Now suddenly, a stranger who smells funny is violating her territory and receiving all your attention. She wonders, "What else is going to change?"

This can be a frightening time, and Kitty needs reassurance. If possible, bring home something that smells like the new cat—a sock or piece of paper he's touched—and leave it in the house for Resident Kitty to find. Let your kitten get used to the idea before you ever bring the strange cat home.

Then, have somebody else bring New Cat into the house in a carrier. That way, your resident feline won't blame you. Separate the cats, placing the New Cat in a room by himself with all his kitty accouterments, and close the door. Resident Kitty still has the run of the rest of the house, which tells her only a portion of her territory has been violated.

Meanwhile, don't make a fuss over the new cat. It should be business as usual while the pair sniff each other from beneath the door. Let them hiss and growl; it's natural cat behavior.

Once Resident Kitty is no longer hissing before the door, try petting the new cat with a mitten or sock, then dropping the scented item somewhere in the house for her to find. You're letting the two very gradually become acquainted so that by the time the door is open they're already used to each other's smell and presence.

Finally, open the door. Don't force them to meet; they'll take care of introductions on their own time. Try feeding them during their first face-to-face so that they'll be disrupted and not pay as much attention. Feed them at opposite ends of the room; they'll be so busy eating they won't have time to pout. Above all, don't make a big deal out of the event. A bit of posturing, hissing and growling is to be expected. After all, they've got to determine who is going to be Top Cat.

Introductions may take time, but friendships are sure to follow.

Sometimes it helps to make the two cats smell alike. Try bathing them both in the same shampoo. Encouraging them to play together is also helpful: get several toys, and let the games begin.

As long as they don't actually engage in a pitched battle, let the pair sort out their own differences. Until they've accepted each other, you may want to keep New Cat in his room when you aren't around to supervise.

Some cats are very accepting and welcome a new feline with little fuss. Others must vent and posture. With patience and time, they should come to terms and develop a feline friendship or, at least, learn to tolerate each other.

Canine Companionship

Despite nasty rumors to the contrary, cats and dogs often get along famously. If they are raised together, cats welcome relationships with canines as a matter of course. Since dogs tend to look to humans for guidance, Poochie usually follows your lead. If you like and accept the kitten, then chances are he will, too.

When introducing kittens to dogs for the first time, please keep in mind that there is a language barrier. In fact, certain canine and feline signals have opposite meanings. For instance, Poochie's wagging behind is a friendly invitation, while a cat's flailing tail expresses anger and excitement. Kitty raises her paw as a warning that a swat is imminent, but that same signal invites canine play. Throwing herself on her back readies feline claws for attack, yet is a canine sign of submission. So be patient; it takes time for both canines and felines to learn each other's language.

Cats and dogs can get along famously, especially if they're raised together.

Many of the same techniques used to introduce another cat will smooth canine meetings. If you already have an adult dog, confine him to one room with a child's gate when you first bring home your kitten. Let them meet by sniffing through the gate or at the bottom of the door. Sometimes, friendships are born immediately, but often it takes time.

SUPERVISE THE STRANGERS

Never leave a dog unsupervised with a small kitten, since accidents can happen no matter how good the dog is. Keep Poochie on a leash whenever the kitten is in the room, until you are sure how the two respond to each other. If the dog is being too aggressive or teasing the kitten, some remedial canine obedience training is needed. And if your kitten is antagonizing the dog, you may need to keep your squirt bottle handy. No bullies allowed!

These two are fast friends already.

Introductions to puppies are easiest, since they're closer to the same size and hopefully haven't learned to be aggressive toward cats. First, confine your kitten to one room, and let the puppy investigate his new home. Then switch, placing the puppy in the room, and allowing your kitten to sniff and smell where he's been.

Introduce the pair with Poochie in a carrier, behind a baby gate barrier, or on a leash under your direct control. Don't make a fuss; just let your kitten investigate Poochie at her own pace.

After a few days of this limited contact, allow them in the same room. Be sure there are escape routes for each so that Poochie can hide in his carrier or Kitty can leap out of reach up a cat tree. Unless they get too aggressive with each other, let Kitty hiss and Poochie yap until they come to terms. Obedience training helps teach puppies acceptable behavior. Before long, the puppy and your kitten should be fast friends, and will grow up together sharing a bed and grooming each other.

Bringing Home a Baby

Cats approach new people and situations cautiously and with respect.

One of the happiest times for you—and potentially confusing times for your cat—is when you bring home a new baby. But cats do not automatically dis-

like babies, neither do they try to suffocate them. Do everyone a favor: Put aside myths, and address reality.

Yes, baby movements and sounds may trigger feline pouncing or batting at a waving little hand. But your kitten isn't being mean; she's just reacting with normal feline reflexes.

And banning Kitty's interaction with Baby doesn't fix anything.

Let Kitty Participate

Above all, *do not* exclude your kitten from this important event. Problems arise when concerned parents whisk Baby into the nursery and lock the door. Now Kitty's shut out of her own territory. From her point of view, you've brought home a tiny being who smells funny, sounds funny, and moves funny, and who seems neither feline nor human. The unexplained is scary and potentially dangerous, so Kitty becomes defensive or even aggressive. She really gets her tail in a knot when all your cherished attention is showered on the interloper. And if you panic every time she walks near the nursery, you encourage problems.

To diffuse difficulties before they develop, slowly acclimatize Kitty ahead of time. Wear baby powder and lotion to help her become familiar with the scents. Record cooing and crying baby sounds, and play the tape for your feline.

EASY DOES IT

Prepare the nursery gradually rather than all at once, painting the room one time and bringing in new furniture another. Allow your kitten to inspect the nursery and perhaps rub against the new crib to leave her scent so that she'll feel more comfortable there.

To keep Kitty away from off-limits areas, like inside the crib, set harmless booby traps such as empty soda cans that make a loud noise when they're knocked over. She will decide it's not such a great nest after all, yet she won't associate the decision with you shouting at her.

Once Baby is born, bring home something the infant has worn, perhaps a tiny tee shirt or cap, and set it out for Kitty to discover and investigate on her own. When you first bring Baby home, don't make a fuss. Simply sit down with Baby in your arms, and wait for Kitty to greet you. Cats are generally good with babies; they approach new situations cautiously and with respect. Let Kitty sniff your baby's things, and if she's calm, let her smell Baby's hands or feet. Don't force the issue; Kitty may decide to hide for a while. Allow your kitten to set her own pace, and encourage and praise her when she returns for introductions.

As long as Kitty knows what this odd new creature is, that Baby is no threat and that Kitty will still get lots of quality attention, there should be no problem. She should be allowed in the nursery when you are there to supervise. Include her in baby activities: talk to her while you're changing diapers, and, perhaps, pet her while Baby is nursing. Kitty will soon associate Baby with positive attention for herself as well.

Meeting Strangers

Learning about different people is easiest for young kittens. But even older kitties are accepting when they are allowed to get to know the new person slowly.

The first rule is: Don't try too hard. Children in particular often want to catch Kitty and play dress-up on first meeting. Don't force a fearful cat, or she will defend herself. Respect goes both ways, so don't inflict ill-mannered children on your kitten. Even with adult strangers, let your kitten make the first move, and always provide her with a safe place to which she can retreat.

A parrot and a kitten would seem the unlikliest of friends— but remember The Owl and the Pussycat.

Associate the new person with positive things. Have visitors sit on the floor, Kitty-level, and engage her in a game. Strangers score points by bringing her a toy or taking over dinner duty and feeding her. Have strangers leave behind a glove or scarf for her to sniff thoroughly at her leisure.

Introductions to males when Kitty has only been around women (and vice versa) can be problematic.

We'll assume your significant other likes cats and wants a good relationship (the alternative is a whole other book). Again, slow is the way to go.

Bring in a tape recording of your intended's voice, and leave his/her cologne-scented belongings around. Associate his/her visits with good things: playtime, meals, grooming or other positive attention. By the time you move in together, the one-time stranger should be feeding Kitty, and she should be demanding attention from him/her, too.

With careful planning, strangers can become friends your kitten will welcome. But remember, you are the most important part of your kitten's life. She loves you and considers you a member of her feline family.

By learning about the enchanting world of cats, you'll come to appreciate your kitten even more. Cherish the special kitten who now shares your life. Kittenhood creates wondrous memories and paves the way for a lifetime of happy adventures together.

part four

Beyond
the
Basics

chapter 12

Recommended Reading

Books

ABOUT HEALTH CARE

Carlson, Delbert, DVM, and James Griffin, MD. *Cat Owner's Home Veterinary Handbook.* New York: Howell Book House, 1983.

Hawcroft, Tim, BVSc. (Hons), MACVs. *First Aid for Cats: The Essential Quick-Reference Guide.* New York: Howell Book House, 1994.

Humphries, Jim, DVM. *Dr. Jim's Animal Clinic for Cats: What People Want to Know.* New York: Howell Book House, 1994.

McGinnis, Terri. *Well Cat Book.* New York: Random House, 1993.

Pitcairn, Richard. *Dr. Pitcairn's Guide to Natural Health for Dogs and Cats.* Emmaus, PA: Rodale Press, 1982.

ABOUT CAT SHOWS

Vella, Carolyn M., and John J. McGonagle, Jr. *In the Spotlight.* New York: Howell Book House, 1990.

ABOUT TRAINING AND BEHAVIOR

Bohnenkamp, Gwen (of the Center for Applied Animal Behavior in San Francisco). Cat training/behavior booklets. James & Kenneth Publishers, 2140 Shattuck Ave. #2406, Berkeley, CA 94704. (510) 658-8588. Order from the publisher.

Biting & Scratching
Cat Training
Household Destruction
Hyperactivity
Litterbox Training
Social Problems

Eckstein, Warren and Fay. *How to Get Your Cat to Do What You Want.* New York: Villard Books, 1990.

Fogle, Bruce, DVM, MRCVs. *The Cat's Mind: Understanding Your Cat's Behavior.* New York: Howell Book House, 1992.

Johnson, Pam (Feline Behavior Consultant). *Twisted Whiskers: Solving Your Cat's Behavior Problems.* Freedom, CA: The Crossing Press, 1994.

Kunkle, Paul. *How to Toilet Train Your Cat.* New York: Workman Publishers, 1991.

Whiteley, E. H. *Understanding and Training Your Cat or Kitten.* New York: Crown Publishing Group, 1994.

Wright, John C., MA, Ph.D., and Judy Wright Lashnits. *Is Your Cat Crazy? Behavior Problems and Solutions from the Casebook of a Cat Therapist.* New York: Macmillan, 1994.

ABOUT BREEDING

Gilbertson, Elaine. *Feline Affair: Guide to Raising and Breeding Purebred Cats.* New York: Alpine Publishing, 1993.

Moore, Anne S. *Breeding Purebred Cats.* Bellevue, MD: Abraxas Publishers, 1981.

GENERAL TITLES

Alderton, David. *Eyewitness Handbook of Cats.* New York: Dorling Kindersley, 1993.

Altman, Roberta. *The Quintessential Cat: A Connoisseur's Guide to the Cat in History, Art, Literature, and Legend.* New York: Macmillan, 1994.

Becker, Suzy. *All I Need to Know I Learned From My Cat.* New York: Workman Publishing Company, 1990.

Bohnenkamp, Gwen. *From the Cat's Point of View.* San Francisco: Perfect Paws (order from publisher, as described earlier).

Camuti, Louis. *All My Patients Are Under the Bed: Memoirs of a Cat Doctor.* New York: Fireside Books, 1980.

Caras, Roger A. *A Cat Is Watching: A Look at the Way Cats See Us.* New York: Simon & Schuster, 1989.

Edney, Andrew. *ASPCA Complete Cat Care Manual.* New York: Houghton Mifflin, 1993.

Fox, Dr. Michael. *Supercat: Raising the Perfect Feline Companion.* New York: Howell Book House, 1990.

Fox, Dr. Michael W. *Understanding Your Cat.* New York: St. Martin's Press, 1974.

Gebhart, Richard. *The Complete Cat Book.* New York: Howell Book House, 1995.

Hammond, Sean, and Carolyn Usrey. *How to Raise a Sane and Healthy Cat.* New York: Howell Book House, 1994.

Hawcroft, Tim, BVSC. (Hons), MACVSc. *The Howell Book of Cat Care.* New York: Howell Book House, 1991.

Holland, Barbara. *Secrets of the Cat: Its Lore, Legend, and Lives.* New York: Ballantine Books, 1989.

Jankowski, Connie. *Adopting Cats and Kittens.* New York: Howell Book House, 1993.

Kelsey-Wood, Dennis. *Atlas of Cats of the World.* Neptune, NJ: TFH, 1990.

Lawson, Tony, and Paté Lawson. *The Cat-Lover's Cookbook.* Pownal, VT: Storey Communications, 1986.

Mallone, John. *The 125 Most Asked Questions About Cats (and the Answers).* New York: William Morrow and Company, Inc., 1992.

Reynolds, Rick and Martha. *Cat Nips.* New York: Berkley Books, 1992.

Shojai, Amy. *The Cat Companion: The History, Culture, and Everyday Life of the Cat.* New York: Mallard Press, 1992.

Siegal, Mordecai, ed. *Cornell Book of Cats.* New York: Villard Books, 1990.

Thomas, Elizabeth Marshall. *Tribe of the Tiger.* New York: Simon & Schuster, 1994.

Wright, John C., Ph.D., and Judi Write Lashnits. *Is Your Cat Crazy? Solutions from the Casebook of a Cat Therapist.* New York: Macmillan, 1994.

Wright, Michael, and Sally Walders (eds.). *The Book of the Cat.* New York: Summit Books, 1980.

Magazines, Newsletters and Catalogs

Animal Watch (published by the ASPCA). 424 E. 92nd St., New York, NY 10128 (212-876-7700)

Cat Fanciers' Almanac. P.O. Box 1005, Manasquan, NJ 08736-1005 (908-528-9797)

Cat Fanciers' Newsletter. 304 Hastings, Redlands, CA 92373

Cat Fancy. P.O. Box 6050, Mission Viejo, CA 92690 (714-855-8822)

Catnip (Newsletter of Tufts University Medical Center). P.O. Box 420014, Palm Coast, FL 32142-0014 (800-829-0926)

CATS. P.O. Box 290037, Port Orange, FL 32129 (904-788-2770)

Cat World International. P.O. Box 35635, Phoenix, AZ 85069 (602-995-1822)

Just Cats. Box 1831, New Fairfield, CT 06812 (203-746-6760)

Meow (Newsletter of the Cat Writer's Association), Charlene Smith, ed. P.O. Box 351, Trilby, FL 33593-0351 (904-583-3744).

Pawprints. P.O. Box 833, North Hollywood, CA 91603 (818-360-4068).

Videos

"Kittens to Cats Video," produced by Pet Avision, Inc. Order from producer: P.O. Box 102, Morgantown, WV 26507 (800-822-2988).

"Video Catnip," sights and sounds of birds and squirrels, produced by Pet Avision, Inc. Order from producer—address and phone number above.

chapter 13

Resources

Cat Registries

The following organizations perform various functions for their members. Their main function is to register cats and record their lineage. Among other duties, the registries charter clubs, regulate various aspects of show administration, approve and publish breed standards, recognize new breeds, and put out several publications each year.

American Association of Cat Enthusiasts
P.O. Box 213
Pine Brook, NJ 07058
(610)916-2079

American Cat Association
8101 Katherine Ave.
Panorama City, CA 91402
(818)782-6080

American Cat Fanciers' Association, Inc.
P.O. Box 203
Point Lookout, MO 65726
(417)334-5430

Cat Fanciers' Association
P.O. Box 1005
Manasquan, NJ 08736-1005
(908)528-9797
(The CFA is the largest registry of pedigreed cats in the world.)

Cat Fanciers' Federation, Inc.
P.O. Box 661
Gratis, OH 45330
(513)787-9009

Happy Household Pet Cat Club
P.O. Box 334
Rome, NY 13442-0334
(513)984-1841

The International Cat Association
P.O. Box 2684
Harlingen, TX 78551
(210)428-8046

United Cat Federation
5510 Ptolemy Way
Mira Loma, CA 91752
(714)685-7896

Humane and Advocacy Groups

Alley Cat Allies
P.O. Box 397
Mount Ranier, MD 20712
(Provides assistance for stray cats)

American Humane Association
Animal Protection Division
63 Iverness Drive East
Englewood, CO 80112
(303)792-9900

American Society for the Prevention of Cruelty to Animals (ASPCA)
424 E. 92nd St.
New York, NY 10128
(212)876-7700

Delta Society
321 Burnett Ave. South, 3rd Floor
Renton, WA 98055-2569
(206)226-7357
(Promotes the human-animal bond)

Friends of Cats
15587 Old Highway 80
El Cahor, CA 92021
(619)561-0361

The Fund for Animals
200 W. 57th St.
New York, NY 10021
(212)246-2096

Humane Society of the United States
2100 L St., NW
Washington, DC 20037
(202)452-1100

I Love Cats
950 Third Ave., 16th Floor
New York, NY 10022-2705
(212)628-7100

Morris Animal Foundation
45 Inverness Drive
East Englewood, CO 80112-5480
(800)243-2345

Pets for Patient Progress
P.O. Box 143
Crystal Lake, IL 60039-9143
(815)455-0990

Pets for People
Call the animal shelter in your area or
(314)982-3028 for information

POWARS (Pet Owners with AIDS/ARC Resource Service, Inc.)
1674 Broadway
Suite 7A
New York, NY 10019
(212)246-6307

Tree House Animal Foundation, Inc.
1212 West Carmen Ave.
Chicago, IL 60640-2999
(312)784-5488

Special Interest

Cat Writers' Association, Inc.
Amy Shojai, president
800 S. 1417, #213
Sherman, TX 75090

NOTES

NOTES

NOTES

Printed in the USA
CPSIA information can be obtained
at www.ICGtesting.com
JSHW072028140824
68134JS00044B/3832